daybook, *n.* a book in which the events of the day are recorded; *specif.* a journal or diary

DAYBOOK
of Critical Reading and Writing

FRAN CLAGGETT

LOUANN REID

RUTH VINZ

Great Source Education Group
a Houghton Mifflin Company
Wilmington, Massachusetts

www.greatsource.com

The Authors

Fran Claggett, currently an educational consultant for schools throughout the country and teacher at Sonoma State University, taught high school English for more than thirty years. She is author of several books, including *Drawing Your Own Conclusions: Graphic Strategies for Reading, Writing, and Thinking* (1992) and *A Measure of Success* (1996).

Louann Reid taught junior and senior high school English, speech, and drama for nineteen years and currently teaches courses for future English teachers at Colorado State University. Author of numerous articles and chapters, her first books were *Learning the Landscape* and *Recasting the Text* with Fran Claggett and Ruth Vinz (1996).

Ruth Vinz, currently a professor and director of English education at Teachers College, Columbia University, taught in secondary schools for twenty-three years. She is author of several books and numerous articles that discuss teaching and learning in the English classroom as well as a frequent presenter, consultant, and co-teacher in schools throughout the country.

Printed in the United States of America

International Standard Book Number: 0-669-46435-X

1 2 3 4 5 6 7 8 9 10 - RRDW - 05 04 03 02 01 00 99 98

TABLE OF CONTENTS

3

4

Focus/Strategy	Lesson	Author/Literature

5

Angles of Literacy

Reading means more than opening a book and trying to figure out an author's message. Reading involves interpreting a story, poem, play, or essay by thinking about it in several ways. Just as you read a person by focusing on particular actions, gestures, and physical characteristics, you read literature in more than one way.

Some angles for making sense of what you read include writing questions and highlighting as you read; making connections to other stories that are related to the ones being told; examining the perspectives; analyzing the author's use of language and craft; and understanding how an author's life figures in his or her writing. These are not the only strategies you will need when reading, but you will find them helpful for understanding what you read.

To learn to interact with what you are reading, you need to **annotate**—that is, underline or circle key words, images, or phrases. As you read, make marginal notes about any ideas, impressions, or questions that strike you. These initial responses will help you focus on what it is you are reacting to. Below, you can see one reader's annotations on Philip Larkin's poem "Mother, Summer, I."

Why does the mother feel as she does?—perhaps she had a really bad life and now when things are going well, it makes her suspicious.

This poem seems to be about a mother who always looks for the negative in life. The son seems to inherit that same feeling because he thinks that if things seem perfect, there may be trouble ahead.

Mother, Summer, I
Philip Larkin

My mother, who hates thunderstorms,
Holds up each summer day and (shakes)
It out suspiciously, lest swarms
Of grape-dark clouds are lurking there;
But when the August weather breaks
And rains begin, and brittle frost   *Mother*
Sharpens the bird-abandoned air,
Her worried summer look is lost.

And I her son, though summer-born
And summer-loving, none the less
Am easier when the leaves are gone;
Too often summer days appear
Emblems of perfect happiness   *Son*
I can't confront: I must await
A time less bold, less rich, less clear:
An autumn more appropriate.

key part!

She is rather like my grandmother who is always saying that anything good will be followed by bad news. The writer helps us see that by using dark images, storm, and cold to describe how the mother sees Summer.

Add two annotations of your own. Then, discuss the poem with a partner, commenting on its meaning for you. Describe your general thoughts and reactions. Remember that working with others is a useful reading strategy. As you finish your conversation, discuss how your understanding of the poem was influenced by your partner's views.

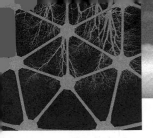

Now read "Far Out" and try your hand at annotating.

Far Out
Philip Larkin

Beyond the bright cartoons
Are darker spaces where
Small cloudy nests of stars
Seem to float on the air.

These have no proper names:
Men out alone at night
Never look up at them
For guidance or delight,

For such evasive dust
Can make so little clear:
Much less is known than not,
More far than near.

11

●◆ Write a paragraph describing your interpretation of the poem after your initial reading and response.

Active readers annotate the text, recording their reactions, questions, and other comments in the margins.

Two Story Connections

Stories in literature exist in several varieties. One type is told explicitly in the literary work. A second type is implied, not told directly but hinted at. With this second type, you imagine and fill in the details of a story for yourself. For example, you may speculate on a character's motivations or imagine an important event that caused the character to react in a certain way. It is important to connect the stories being told or implied to your own personal stories. Look back at "Mother, Summer, I" and consider the connections written by one reader. Then look for story connections in "Ambulances."

Response notes

Ambulances
Philip Larkin

Closed like confessionals, they thread
Loud noons of cities, giving back
None of the glances they absorb.
Light glossy grey, arms on a plaque,
They come to rest at any kerb:
All streets in time are visited.

Then children strewn on steps or road,
Or women coming from the shops
Past smells of different dinners, see
A wild white face that overtops
Red stretcher-blankets momently
As it is carried in and stowed,

And sense the solving emptiness
That lies just under all we do,
And for a second get it whole,
So permanent and blank and true.
The fastened doors recede. *Poor soul,*
They whisper at their own distress;

For borne away in deadened air
May go the sudden shut of loss
Round something nearly at an end,
And what cohered in it across
The years, the unique random blend
Of families and fashions, there

At last begin to loosen. Far
From the exchange of love to lie
Unreachable inside a room
The traffic parts to let go by
Brings closer what is left to come,
And dulls to distance all we are.

●◆ Write a few sentences describing the main story of this poem. Why do you think Larkin is telling this story?

●◆ List a few examples of possible stories that could be developed from the story that is told. For example, one might be about the "women coming from the shops." A second might be about one of the ambulance drivers. List some other possibilities.

●◆ Briefly describe a personal experience that you were reminded of after reading "Ambulances." Describe the connection you made. Share your description with a partner.

Readers can connect all the stories in a work of literature to their own life experiences.

Shifting Perspectives

Your interpretation of an event in your life may take on a different meaning when you see it through someone else's eyes. Good readers get a different **perspective** by examining or changing the **point of view**. Other ways to get a different perspective include, determining more than one way of interpreting a situation or character, switching **genre**, and creating "what if" speculations.

•❖ Reread the poem "Mother, Summer, I." What do you know about the speaker?

•❖ What might be different if the mother told her own story? Write a new version of the poem, from her perspective. Model your poem on the sentence structure and phrases of the original. Your poem can be shorter than "Mother, Summer, I."

Discuss with a partner what stands out for each of you about the mother's point of view. How does the **imagery** used to describe the mother's perspective compare with that used to present the son's?

●◆ Reread Larkin's poem "Ambulances." Write a few sentences about how you might react to the poem if:

• The title were different. Think of another title and discuss how the title changes the emphasis or interpretation.

Title: ....

Explanation: ....

....

....

....

....

• You were an ambulance driver.

....

....

....

....

....

• You were in an accident yourself and benefited from ambulance service.

....

....

....

....

Examine a piece of literature from several perspectives. Changes in point of view or "what if" speculations can change the interpretation of what you are reading.

Four Language and Craft

In reading poetry, it is important to focus on the ways in which language shapes and emphasizes meaning. In the annotations to "Mother, Summer, I," the reader noted how Larkin's language helped support the mother's attitudes. Focus on imagery as you read "Street Lamps." Begin by noting the particular images used.

Response notes

Street Lamps
Philip Larkin

When night slinks, like a puma, down the sky,
    And the bare, windy streets echo with silence,
Street lamps come out, and lean at corners, awry,
    Casting black shadows, oblique and intense;
So they burn on, impersonal, through the night,
    Hearing the hours slowly topple past
Like cold drops from a glistening stalactite,
    Until grey planes splinter the gloom at last;
Then they go out.

        I think I noticed once
    —T'was morning—one sole street-lamp still bright-lit,
Which, with a senile grin, like an old dunce,
    Vied the blue sky, and tried to rival it;
And, leering pallid though its use was done,
Tried to cast shadows contrary to the sun.

16

List key images in the chart below. Decide what each image means, and then determine how the individual images contribute to the overall meaning of the poem.

Image	Meaning	Contribution to Overall Meaning
night slinks, like a puma	dark and predatory	showing dark to contrast with light

●◆ Another way to study the imagery is to translate the words into visual sketches. In the following boxes, sketch a series of pictures that represent the imagery that is the strongest for you in "Street Lamps."

●◆ Now, use the chart and your sketches to help you write about how the imagery in "Street Lamps" contributes to the overall meaning of the poem.

Examining the use of language gives you clues about what the writer has chosen to emphasize and helps you see how craft supports meaning.

Five

Focus on the Writer

Focusing on one work gives only a limited picture of an author. You should study the author's life, read multiple works by the author, and analyze the subject matter, themes, and style. Consider the following excerpt from Philip Larkin's "Notebooks." Record in the response notes any connections you make between this passage and Larkin's poetry.

---

from "Notebooks" by Philip Larkin

← *Response notes* →

By the time I knew it, my father worked all day and shut himself away reading in the evening, or else gardened. My mother constantly toiled at "running the house," a task that was always beyond her, even with the aid of the resident maid and daily help. My sister, whose qualities of literal-mindedness and fantasy spinning had infuriated my father until he made her life a misery, did not have many friends and endured, I should say, a pallid existence until she took up art and even then day classes at Midland Art School did not lead to the excitement they should have. I don't think my father liked working or gardening, I don't think my mother liked keeping house, I don't think my sister liked living at home. Yet they all seemed powerless to do anything about it. There was a curious tense boredom about the house; it was not a bad house, but the furniture was uninteresting, except for my father's books. It was not a house where anyone called unexpectedly, for my father had no friends—at least, I couldn't name anyone who was a friend as I understand the word.

However, the trouble wasn't the house but the individuals in it. My mother, as time went on, began increasingly to complain of her dreary life, her inability to run the house, and the approach of war. I suppose her age had something to do with it, but the monotonous whining monologue she treated my father to before breakfast, and all of us at mealtimes, resentful, self-pitying, full of funk and suspicion, must have remained in my mind as something I mustn't *under any circumstances* risk encountering again. Once she sprang up from the table announcing her intention to commit suicide. I never left the house without the sense of walking into a cooler, cleaner, saner and pleasanter atmosphere, and, if I had not made friends outside, life would have been scarcely tolerable.

❧ How does the information you learned about Larkin's life help you understand "Mother, Summer, I" and the subject or imagery in any of the other Larkin poems?

18

Another way to understand more about an author's life and work is to read the author's reflections on writing. In his "Notebooks," Larkin describes how he came to be a writer. In high school, he knew that he was unremarkable except for one asset:

from "Notebooks" by Philip Larkin

What I was going to be praised and rewarded for—if anything—was writing. It certainly wasn't going to be languages or science, both of which we started that year, nor sport, for which advancing age, with its shortening sight and stiffening joints and increasing physical fastidiousness was rapidly unfitting me, nor was I going to do anything requiring confidence and a speaking voice. On the other hand, I was getting used to hearing my essays read out in class, and to coming top in English examinations by unarguable margins. Words were my element, though I no more understood them, in the parts of speech or philological senses, than a seal understands the water it lives in.

←—Response notes—→

List three phrases from each poem that you think demonstrate Larkin's belief that words are his "element."

Quotes from Poems	What the Quote Demonstrates
"Mother, Summer, I" "grape-dark clouds"	good at creating visual imagery
"Far Out"	
"Ambulances"	
"Street Lamps"	

19

●◆ Design a cover for a book that compiles excerpts from Larkin's "Notebooks" and his poems. Title the book and sketch a cover design on the front. On the back, give the prospective reader pertinent information along with an introductory sample of lines from Larkin's poetry.

Examining a writer in depth—the author's life and work and what the author or others say about the work—is one way to extend your understanding of a literary selection.

Building an Interpretation

When you read a story, one of the first impulses is to ask: "What is this about?" You might also ask: "What is happening that keeps me interested? What makes me think the story is worth reading?" Each of these questions gets at different levels of meaning in the story. The first question hints at the need for a reader to understand what is going on. The second and third signal the reader's interest in finding meaningful connections to the events, ideas, or questions that the story raises.

Meaning comes from the ways in which you build and develop an interpretation. This requires that you look closely at a combination of characteristics and impressions of the subject and the craft of the story. As you read, keep in mind how the writer selected and arranged the details and events in ways that prompt you to find and to create meaning from what you read.

One Subject and Story Meaning

With a story, a writer provides you with a subject. By reading it you create the meaning. Your meaning is based on your experiences and attitudes. In the novel *Paddy Clarke Ha Ha Ha*, Roddy Doyle tells the story of a young Irish boy. On the first reading, try to get a sense of the whole episode.

← *Response notes* →

from *Paddy Clarke Ha Ha Ha* by Roddy Doyle

The teacher we had before Henno, Miss Watkins, brought in a tea-towel with the Proclamation of Independence on it because it was fifty years after 1916. It had the writing part in the middle and the seven men who'd signed it around the sides. She stuck it up over the blackboard and let us up to see it one by one. Some of the boys blessed themselves in front of it.

—*Nach bhfuil sé go h'álainn* [Isn't it lovely], lads? she kept saying after every couple of boys went past.

—*Tá* [Yes], we said back.

I looked at the names at the bottom. Thomas J. Clarke was the first one. Clarke, like my name.

Miss Watkins got her *bata* [stick] and read the proclamation out for us and pointed at each word.

—In this supreme hour the Irish nation must, by its valour and discipline, and by the readiness of its children to sacrifice themselves for the common good, prove itself worthy of the august destiny to which it is called. Signed on behalf of the provisional government, Thomas J. Clarke, Seán MacDiarmada, Thomas MacDonagh, P. H. Pearse, Eamonn Ceannt, James Connolly, Joseph Plunkett.

Miss Watkins started clapping, so we did as well. We started laughing. She stared at us and we stopped but we kept clapping.

I turned back to James O'Keefe.

—Thomas Clarke is my granda. Pass it on.

Miss Watkins rapped the blackboard with the bata.

—*Seasaígí suas.* [Stand up.]

She made us march in step beside our desks.

—*Clé—deas—clé deas—clé—* [Left—right—left right—left—]

The walls of the prefab wobbled. The prefabs were behind the school. You could crawl under them. The varnish at the front of them was all flaky because of the sun; you could peel it off. We didn't get a room in the proper school, the cement one, until a year after this, when we got changed to Henno. We loved marching. We could feel the boards hopping under us. We put so much effort into slamming our feet down that we couldn't keep in time. She made us do this a couple of times a day, when she said we were looking lazy.

While we marched this time Miss Watkins read the proclamation.

—Irishmen and Irishwomen: In the name of God and of the dead generations from which she receives her old tradition of nationhood, Ireland, through us, summons her children to her flag and strikes for her freedom.

from ***Paddy Clarke Ha Ha Ha*** by R o d d y D o y l e

She had to stop. It wasn't proper marching any more. She hit the blackboard.

← *Response notes* →

—*Suígí síos.* [Sit down.]

She looked annoyed and disappointed.

Kevin put his hand up.

—Miss?

Sea? [Yes.]

—Paddy Clarke said his granda's Thomas Clarke on the tea-towel, Miss.

—Did he now?

—Yes, Miss.

—Patrick Clarke.

—Yes, Miss.

—Stand up till we see you.

It took ages for me to get out of my desk.

—Your grandfather is Thomas Clarke?

I smiled.

—Is he?

—Yes, Miss.

—This man here?

She pointed at Thomas Clarke in one of the corners of the tea-towel. He looked like a granda.

—Yes, Miss.

—Where does he live, tell us?

—Clontarf, Miss.

—Where?

—Clontarf, Miss.

—Come up here to me, Patrick Clarke.

The only noise was me on the floorboards.

She pointed to a bit of writing under Thomas Clarke's head.

—Read that for us, Patrick Clarke.

—Ex–eh–executed by the British on 3 May, 1916.

—What does Executed mean, Dermot Grimes who's picking his nose and doesn't think I can see him?

—Kilt, Miss.

—That's right. And this is your grandfather who lives in Clontarf, is it, Patrick Clarke?

—Yes, Miss.

I pretended to look at the picture again.

—I'll ask you again, Patrick Clarke. Is this man your grandfather?

—No, Miss.

She gave me three on each hand.

When I got back to the desk I couldn't put the seat down; my hands couldn't do anything. James O'Keefe pushed the seat down for me with his foot. It made a bang; I thought she'd get me again. I put my hands under my legs. I didn't crouch: she wouldn't let us. The pain was like my hands had dropped off; it would soon become more of a wet sting. The palms were beginning to sweat like mad. There was no noise. I looked over at Kevin. I grinned but my teeth

chattered. I saw Liam turn round at the front of the row, waiting for Kevin to look his way, waiting to grin for him.

I liked my Granda Clarke, much more than Granda Finnegan. Granda Clarke's wife, my Grandma, wasn't alive any more.

—She's up in heaven, he said,—having a great time.

He gave me half a crown when we went to see him or when he came to see us. He once came on a bike.

I was messing through the drawers in the sideboard one night when Mart and Market was on the television. The bottom drawer was so full of photographs that when I was sliding the drawer back in some of the photographs on the top of the pile fell out the back onto the floor under the sideboard. I got them out from under there. One of them was of Granda and Grandma Clarke. We hadn't been to his house in ages.

—Dad?

—Yes, son?

—When are we going to Granda Clarke's?

My da looked like he'd lost something, then found it, but it wasn't what he'd wanted.

He sat up. He looked at me for a while.

—Granda Clarke's dead, he said. —Do you not remember?

—No.

I couldn't.

He picked me up.

24

Every story concerns itself with some subject—growing up, confronting a difficult situation, finding a new friend, and so on. The meaning of a story should not be confused with a story's subject; meaning comes from the interpretation of details in the story. The subject is simply what the story is about.

➥ Describe the subject of Doyle's story as you understand it.

●◆ Now explore the meaning you find behind the specific situation and characters presented. Answer the following questions using examples from the story to illustrate your points:

1. How do the incidents and characters compare with your own experiences? How do these comparisons affect the ways you respond to the episode?

....

....

....

....

....

....

2. What techniques does Doyle employ—for example, point of view, descriptions, images, humor—to influence your attitude toward the events and characters?

....

....

....

....

....

3. What ideas seem significant in the story?

....

....

....

....

....

....

Readers need to compare the story subject to their own lives, examine how the writer develops the subject, and generalize from the story events in order to build an interpretation.

Two

Conflict and Story Meaning

Conflict is the backbone of a story. **Conflict** creates the sense that there are good reasons to tell the story. Writers introduce and explore a conflict to make the meaning believable and complex. As you read the opening of William Trevor's "The Piano Tuner's Wives," look for the first hints of possible conflicts and how Trevor introduces these.

from "The Piano Tuner's Wives" by William Trevor

←— Response notes —→

Violet married the piano tuner when he was a young man. Belle married him when he was old.

There was a little more to it than that, because in choosing Violet to be his wife the piano tuner had rejected Belle, which was something everyone remembered when the second wedding was announced. "Well, she got the ruins of him anyway," a farmer of the neighborhood remarked, speaking without vindictiveness, stating a fact as he saw it. Others saw it similarly, though most of them would have put the matter differently.

The piano tuner's hair was white and one of his knees became more arthritic with each damp winter that passed. He had once been svelte but was no longer so, and he was blinder than on the day he married Violet — a Thursday in 1951, June 7th. The shadows he lived among now had less shape and less density than those of 1951.

"I will," he responded in the small Protestant church of St Colman, standing almost exactly as he had stood on that other afternoon. And Belle, in her fifty-ninth year, repeated the words her one-time rival had spoken before this altar also. A decent interval had elapsed; no one in the church considered that the memory of Violet had not been honored, that her passing had not been distressfully mourned. ". . . and with all my worldly goods I thee endow," the piano tuner stated, while his new wife thought she would like to be standing beside him in white instead of suitable wine-red. She had not attended the first wedding, although she had been invited. She'd kept herself occupied that day, whitewashing the chicken shed, but even so she'd wept. And tears or not, she was more beautiful—and younger by almost five years—than the bride who so vividly occupied her thoughts as she battled with her jealousy. Yet he had preferred Violet—or the prospect of the house that would one day become hers, Belle told herself bitterly in the chicken shed, and the little bit of money there was, an easement in a blind man's existence. How understandable, she was reminded later on, whenever she saw Violet guiding him as they walked, whenever she thought of Violet making everything work for him, giving him a life. Well, so could she have.

As they left the church the music was by Bach, the organ played by someone else today, for usually it was his task. Groups formed in the small graveyard that was scattered around the small grey building, where the piano tuner's father and mother were buried, with ancestors on his father's side from previous generations. There would

from **"The Piano Tuner's Wives"** by William Trevor

←—Response notes—→

be tea and a few drinks for any of the wedding guests who cared to make the journey to the house, two miles away, but some said goodbye now, wishing the pair happiness. The piano tuner shook hands that were familiar to him, seeing in his mental eye faces that his first wife had described for him. It was the depth of summer, as in 1951, the sun warm on his forehead and his cheeks, and on his body through the heavy wedding clothes. All his life he had known this graveyard, had first felt the letters on the stones as a child, spelling out to his mother the names of his father's family. He and Violet had not had children themselves, though they'd have liked them. He was her child, it had been said, a statement that was an irritation for Belle whenever she heard it. She would have given him children, of that she felt certain.

Conflicts may be external (originating from factors outside) or internal (within the mind) for the characters. Indicate on the chart below which elements of the conflict you consider external and which internal for Belle and for the piano tuner.

Character	Internal/External Conflict?	Reasons I think so
Belle: rejected for Violet	originally external now internal	nature of conflict changed with Violet's death.
Piano tuner:		

27

Share your chart with a partner. As you discuss the various conflicts, consider how they might be important to the overall meaning of the story.

The conflicts presented in a story dramatize key themes that can be interpreted for what they contribute to the overall meaning of a story.

Three

Conveying Meaning Through Tone

The **tone** conveys part of the story's meaning. Clues to the narrator's tone—the attitude toward characters and events—are often found in the narrator's descriptions and emphasis.

●◆ Describe the tone of the following quotes from "The Piano Tuner's Wives." Explain what you think the tone reveals about the story's meaning.

1. "Violet married the piano tuner when he was a young man. Belle married him when he was old."

2. " 'I will,' he responded in the small Protestant church of St. Colman, standing almost exactly as he had stood on that other afternoon."

3. "The piano tuner shook hands that were familiar to him, seeing in his mental eye faces that his first wife had described for him."

4. "She would have given him children, of that she felt certain."

●◆ Write a few sentences about the narrator's tone toward any one subject—a character, the wedding, the guest's attitudes, the past. Explain how Trevor reveals this tone.

●◆ Now describe the subject with a different tone. In a few sentences, have the narrator describe the same details or descriptions in ways that fit the new tone.

Understanding the tone used to describe the subject and characters in a story is one way of developing an interpretation of the story's meaning.

Writers use various types of **imagery** to create the **setting**, events, and characters in a story. Readers study the imagery used and the meaning emphasized by these descriptions. In David Malouf's novel *The Conversations at Curlow Creek*, two characters talk through the night. One is Carney, an Irish convict, who is sentenced to hang at dawn. The other is Adair, a professional soldier who is keeping watch over the prisoner.

from *The Conversations at Curlow Creek* by David Malouf

← *Response notes* →

He [Adair] slept again, and this time what he dreamed he did remember.

He was standing in clear sunlight at the edge of a vast sheet of water, so dazzling with salt and reflected light that he could not see the farther shore and had for a moment to shield his eyes against its blinding throb. He was aware of another presence, close at his side but slightly behind. He felt its heaviness there, but knew he must not turn his head to look or it would vanish, and with it the lake or inland sea and its wash of light, and he too, since he understood that the figure there at his side was himself, a more obscure, endangered self with a history that was his but had somehow been kept secret from him. The tenderness and concern he felt was for both of them.

He knew this country well enough by now to be skeptical of his senses. The lake, with the next step he took, could quite easily shrivel up with a cackle, and there would be in its place only an equally vast expanse of sharp and dazzling stones. Meanwhile, mirage or not, he held it. I have to take the risk, he told himself, and the figure at his side granted assent.

He took a step. The vision held. The great sheet of light exulted, all ripples.

Another.

Again it shivered, shook out lines of light, and he saw now that sea-birds were brooding in the furrows, gulls, and that other birds, waders on long stilts, were either stilled in the shallows or walking in a stately manner, one clawed foot raised, held, then solemnly lowered, in a parade along the shore. Fish heaved in shoals below its smooth and polished surface, great swathes of shadow that suddenly showed silver where their backs broke water and their scales caught the sun. Such plenty!

It is real, he breathed. It is a door in the darkness, a way out. His heart lifted at the thought and there came a clatter, far out, an explosion of wings, and he saw that in the midst of the commotion was a boat, a low dug-out driven by many rowers; far out but rapidly approaching. He stepped forward to call to them. But the moment his breath flew out there was an answering upheaval, as if a sudden wind had struck the lake. Its surface rippled like silk, and the whole weight and light of it was sucked upwards in a single movement that took his breath away; a single, shiningly transparent sack, it was being hauled upwards, as in a theatre, by invisible hands. He tried to shout but

from *The Conversations at Curlow Creek* by David Malouf

was breathless. He reached up, with a terrible tightening of his chest, to pluck it back.

It was moving fast now, like an air-balloon, soaring aloft till it was just a distant, spherical drop, rather milky; then, as the sun struck it, a brilliant speck. Gone, with all its vision, of light, birds, fish, men, rescue. He was choking. At the end of his breath. But the presence at his side was still there, breath labouring, pumping.

He woke, and had the uneasy feeling of having stepped from one dream into another that was even more remote. He laboured to catch his breath. Daniel Carney's one eye was fixed upon him with a savage watchfulness.

"I must have dozed off," he said. It was half a question.

"Yes sir; you did sleep for a bit."

"How long?"

"A minute or two. Maybe less."

A minute or two? Had he really experienced so much in so short a time? Could the mind—out of what rich well?— draw up such bright, such enlarging images, play so powerfully on the nerves, hold out the promise of hopeful issue, of escape from the hard facts of circumstance, only so that some natural or supernatural force could pluck it away again, and all this in the space of a hundred tumultuous heart-beats?

As on many occasions before, he was struck by the difference between minutes as the watch in his pocket might have ticked them off and this other time he carried in his head, which was infinitely expandable and had nothing to do with the movements of either the earth or the sun.

Again he was aware of Carney's gaze upon him, intense, almost predatory, as if he might have news to bring him out of what he had dreamed. News of rescue, was it? Could he know that? Of a rescue that at the last moment had failed? He felt a kind of warning that he should control his thoughts if he did not want them known; that the space they shared was no longer a contained one with fixed walls and a roof, but was open, and in such a way that the normal rules of separation, of one thing being distinct to itself and closed against another, no longer applied.

I am not properly awake, he thought. I was right the first time. I have wakened into another dream.

The first step toward interpreting the meaning of an image is to determine what it causes you to experience. Highlight the images from this episode that creates the strongest sensory responses.

●◆Choose one of passages you marked and explain which word or words in the passage made you experience what Adair was experiencing.

....

....

....

A second step in building an interpretation is examining how particular images contribute to meaning.

●◆ Review the imagery that you marked. Then complete the following assertion.

The imagery in Adair's dream suggests that he

....

....

On the left, list the imagery that offers the strongest support for your interpretation. On the right, explain why the image is important.

Imagery	How It Supports Assertion
"shield his eyes against its blinding throb"	Not wanting to face what is coming

In developing an interpretation, it is important to monitor your responses to the imagery and to examine how particular images emphasize the story's meaning.

Five
Interpreting Meaning

Taking apart the story is another way to begin building an interpretation. Make notes on each of the strategies suggested below to refine your developing interpretation of *The Conversations at Curlow Creek*.

1. Choose a key quote and explain how it helps convey what you see as the overall meaning of the episode. Explain why you think so.

2. Choose a central image that exemplifies a theme in the episode. Explain how it is significant to the characters and events.

33

3. Explain the title. How does it highlight the specific incidents or characters described in the episode?

4. Choose one of the elements of the story—plot, setting, character, or point of view—and explain what this element illustrates about themes and meaning of the episode.

●◆Now develop a short interpretive essay. At its basic level, the word *interpret* means to understand and to explain the meaning. Think about what you would tell someone else about your understanding of this episode from *The Conversations at Curlow Creek*. Act as an interpreter for the ideas that come through for you.

Interpreting involves looking closely at a combination of characteristics and impressions from a story and then piecing together their meaning.

Literary Belief

The basic advice given to every young writer is to "write about what you know." Yet, if every writer followed it, we would not have the rich selection of imaginary fiction that we do. Writers create stories that go beyond a report of real-life incidents. Fiction is "made up." We evaluate stories on whether or not we are led to suspend our critical intelligence and believe in some reality beyond our own. Writers use details—the names of streets, descriptions of weather, or the looks and gestures of characters—to convince us that the world we know is being depicted in the story. The writer has the responsibility to make the characters and events convincing. Edgar Allan Poe once said that stories express our intuitions of reality. A good story persuades us to believe that a world different from our own can exist.

How Readers Come to Believe

Just how does a writer create a story that draws on your willingness to believe? The writer creates a fictional reality, but relies on concrete details to show the characters, setting, and events. As you read an excerpt from a story by the Australian writer Penelope Trevor, notice how the narrator's details help you experience the reality of the situation for nine-year-old Joss.

← Response notes →

from *Listening for Small Sounds* by Penelope Trevor

September winds blow away the grey and the sun rises, yellow, into a blue sky.

Outside Joss feels the spring. In the doll's house it is still winter. She and Misi scavenge in the lanes. Joss picks flowers from honeysuckle bushes that hang over people's back fences. The liquid is watery and not very sweet, weak, like the sunshine.

When Maria goes out, Joss climbs over her back fence and steals three mandarins from a tree in her backyard. She looks for the old man. She wants to give him one but she can't find him. So she goes inside and gives one to her mother.

Her mother is in the bathroom, on her knees leaning over the bathtub, scrubbing. She has rubber gloves on and they're covered in Ajax so Joss peels a mandarin for her. It's a bit green.

"Here Mum." She pops a piece into her mother's mouth. Her mother makes a face.

"Bitter?"

Her mother nods. Joss pops a piece into her own mouth. Her tongue puckers. Her mother puts one hand on the side of the bath and stands up. Joss thinks she's going to rinse the bath out now. But she doesn't. She starts scrubbing the tiles on the wall around the bath. They don't look dirty to Joss.

Joss picks up the spare Wettex and the Ajax from the bathroom floor. She walks over to the basin and shakes some Ajax into the sink. Where the sink has water on it the Ajax turns blue.

Joss wonders about germs. She pushes some Ajax down into the plughole.

"I know how to make a vaccine, Mum."

Her mother doesn't say anything.

"I mean if there was an epidemic or something." Joss shakes some more Ajax into the sink. "You know, like the black plague." She looks at her mother.

"That's nice, dear."

"Do you want me to tell you?"

Her mother turns on the shower to rinse the Ajax off the walls. It runs down into the bath. Joss decides to tell her anyway.

"Just say you'd been sick from something. And then you got better. But everyone else was still sick from it. I'd take a pint of your blood because you'd be a recovered victim. And then I'd put your blood in a

from *Listening for Small Sounds* by Penelope Trevor

← *Response notes* →

jar and tie a rope around the jar and swing it around my head for twenty minutes."

Her mother turns the shower off and stretches.

"When you stop swinging it around it's all separated. There's three layers."

Her mother turns around and lifts up the toilet seat.

"But it's only the top one you need. It's clear and it's the vaccine. And then you just give it to people."

Her mother looks at her and smiles. Joss knows she's trying to think of something to say.

"Where did you learn that?"

"I read it in a book."

"Pass the Ajax, honey."

Joss passes it to her. Her mother takes the long brush and starts to scrub the toilet.

That night Joss walks up to the takeaway Chinese restaurant with Misi. She orders Sweet and Sour Pork and Fried Rice. Her mother doesn't feel like cooking. She says she's not hungry, but she says Joss has to eat.

When Joss gets home her mother is sitting in front of the telly, knitting. One pearl, one plain, one pearl. Her hands do it all by themselves.

37

●◆ Explain how Trevor creates believability. Write a paragraph describing which part of the episode you think is developed most convincingly. Analyze the concrete details that persuaded you to believe in this story's reality.

....

....

....

....

....

....

....

....

....

Share what you wrote with a partner. Compare what episode each of you chose and your reasons for thinking it believable.

Believability in a story develops from concrete details that present events and characters.

Writers' backgrounds, interests, and experiences guide the types of characters and situations they portray in their stories. Nadine Gordimer was born and lives in South Africa. Her novels and stories show the turmoil of life there. How does Gordimer enable you to see and feel South Africa in the following story?

←—Response notes—→

"Comrades" by Nadine Gordimer

As Mrs. Hattie Telford pressed the electronic gadget that deactivates the alarm device in her car a group of youngsters came up behind her. Black. But no need to be afraid; this was not a city street. This was a non-racial enclave of learning, a place where tended flowerbeds and trees bearing botanical identification plates civilized the wild reminder of campus guards and dogs. The youngsters, like her, were part of the crowd loosening into dispersion after a university conference on People's Education. They were the people to be educated; she was one of the committee of white and black activists (convenient generic for revolutionaries, leftists secular and Christian, fellow-travelers and liberals) up on the platform.

—Comrade . . . — She was settling in the driver's seat when one so slight and slim he seemed a figure in profile came up to her window. He drew courage from the friendly lift of the woman's eyebrows above blue eyes, the tilt of her freckled white face: —Comrade, are you going to town?—

No, she was going in the opposite direction, home . . . but quickly, in the spirit of the hall where these young people had been somewhere, somehow present with her (ah no, she with them) stamping and singing Freedom songs, she would take them to the bus station their spokesman named. —Climb aboard!—

The others got in the back, the spokesman beside her. She saw the nervous white of his eyes as he glanced at and away from her. She searched for talk to set them at ease. Questions, of course. Older people always start with questioning young ones. Did they come from Soweto?

They came from Harrismith, Phoneng Location.

She made the calculation: about two hundred kilometres distant. How did they get here? Who told them about the conference?

—We are Youth Congress in Phoneng.—

A delegation. They had come by bus; one of the groups and stragglers who kept arriving long after the conference had started. They had missed, then, the free lunch?

At the back, no one seemed even to be breathing. The spokesman must have had some silent communication with them, some obligation to speak for them created by the journey or by other shared experience in the mysterious bonds of the young—these young.—We are hungry.—And from the back seats was drawn an assent like the suction of air in a compressing silence.

"Comrades" by Nadine Gordimer

←—Response notes—→

She was silent in response, for the beat of a breath or two. These large gatherings both excited and left her overexposed, open and vulnerable to the rub and twitch of the mass shuffling across rows of seats and loping up the aisles, babies' fudge-brown soft legs waving as their napkins are changed on mothers' laps, little girls with plaited loops on their heads listening like old crones, heavy women swaying to chants, men with fierce, unreadably black faces breaking into harmony tender and deep as they sing to God for his protection of Umkhonto weSizwe, as people on both sides have always, everywhere, claimed divine protection for their soldiers, their wars. At the end of a day like this she wanted a drink, she wanted the depraved luxury of solitude and quiet in which she would be restored (enriched, oh yes! by the day) to the familiar limits of her own being.

Hungry. Not for iced whisky and feet up. It seemed she had scarcely hesitated: —Look, I live nearby, come back to my house and have something to eat. Then I'll run you into town. —

—That will be very nice. We can be glad for that. —And at the back the tight vacuum relaxed.

They followed her in through the gate, shrinking away from the dog—she assured them he was harmless but he was large, with a fancy collar by which she held him. She trooped them in through the kitchen because that was the way she always entered her house, something she would not have done if they had been adult, her black friends whose sophistication might lead them to believe the choice of entrance was an unthinking historical slight. As she was going to feed them, she took them not into her living-room with its sofas and flowers but into her dining-room, so that they could sit at table right away. It was a room in confident taste that could afford to be spare: bare floorboards, matching golden wooden ceiling, antique brass chandelier, reed blinds instead of stuffy curtains. An African wooden sculpture represented a lion marvellously released from its matrix in the grain of a Mukwa tree-trunk. She pulled up the chairs and left the four young men while she went back to the kitchen to make coffee and see what there was in the refrigerator for sandwiches. They had greeted the maid, in the language she and they shared, on their way through the kitchen, but when the maid and the lady of the house had finished preparing cold meat and bread, and the coffee was ready, she suddenly did not want them to see that the maid waited on her. She herself carried the heavy tray into the dining-room.

They are sitting round the table, silent, and there is no impression that they stopped an undertone exchange when they heard her approaching. She doles out plates, cups. They stare at the food but their eyes seem focused on something she can't see; something that overwhelms. She urges them—Just cold meat, I'm afraid, but there's chutney if you like it . . . milk everybody? . . . is the coffee too strong, I have a heavy hand, I know. Would anyone like to add some hot water?—

They eat. When she tries to talk to one of the others, he says *Ekskuus*? And she realizes he doesn't understand English, of the

39

white man's languages knows perhaps only a little of that of the
Afrikaners in the rural town he comes from. Another gives his name,
as if in some delicate acknowledgement of the food. —I'm Shadrack
Nsutsha. —She repeats the surname to get it right. But he does not
speak again. There is an urgent exchange of eye-language, and the
spokesman holds out the emptied sugar-bowl to her. —Please.— She
hurries to the kitchen and brings it back refilled. They need
carbohydrate, they are hungry, they are young, they need it, they
burn it up. She is distressed at the inadequacy of the meal and then
notices the fruit bowl, her big copper fruit bowl, filled with apples and
bananas and perhaps there is a peach or two under the grape leaves
with which she likes to complete an edible still life. —Have some fruit.
Help yourselves.—

They are stacking their plates and cups, not knowing what they
are expected to do with them in this room which is a room where
apparently people only eat, do not cook, do not sleep. While they
finish the bananas and apples (Shadrack Nsutsha had seen the single
peach and quickly got there first) she talks to the spokesman, whose
name she has asked for: Dumile. —Are you still at school, Dumile?—
Of course he is not at school—*they* are not at school; youngsters their
age have not been at school for several years, they are the children
growing into young men and women for whom school is a battleground,
a place of boycotts and demonstrations, the literacy of political
rhetoric, the education of revolt against having to live the life their
parents live. They have pompous titles of responsibility beyond
childhood: he is chairman of his branch of the Youth Congress, he was
expelled two years ago—for leading a boycott? Throwing stones at the
police? Maybe burning the school down? He calls it all—quietly,
abstractly, doesn't know many ordinary, concrete words but knows
these euphemisms— "political activity." No school for two years? No.
—So what have you been able to do with yourself, all that time?—

She isn't giving him a chance to eat his apple. He swallows a large
bite, shaking his head on its thin, little-boy neck. —I was inside.
Detained from this June for six months.—

She looks round the others. —And you?—

Shadrack seems to nod slightly. The other two look at her. She
should know, she should have known, it's a common enough answer
from youths like them, their colour. They're not going to be saying
they've been selected for the 1st Eleven at cricket or that they're off
on a student tour to Europe in the school holidays.

The spokesman, Dumile, tells her he wants to study by
correspondence, "get his matric" that he was preparing for two years
ago; two years ago when he was still a child, when he didn't have the
hair that is now appearing on his face, making him a man, taking
away the childhood. In the hesitations, the silences of the table, where
there is nervously spilt coffee among plates of banana skins, there
grows the certainty that he will never get the papers filled in for the
correspondence college, he will never get the two years back. She
looks at them all and cannot believe what she knows: that they,
suddenly here in her house, will carry the AK-47's they only sing

40

"Comrades" by Nadine Gordimer

← Response notes →

about, now, miming death as they sing. They will have a career of wiring explosives to the undersides of vehicles, they will go away and come back through the bush to dig holes not to plant trees to shade home, but to plant land-mines. She can see they have been terribly harmed but cannot believe they could harm. They are wiping their fruit-sticky hands furtively palm against palm.

She breaks the silence; says something, anything.

—How d'you like my lion? Isn't he beautiful? He's made by a Zimbabwean artist, I think the name's Dube.—

But the foolish interruption becomes revelation. Dumile, in his gaze—distant, lingering, speechless this time—reveals what has overwhelmed them. In this room, the space, the expensive antique chandelier, the consciously simple choice of reed blinds, the carved lion: all are on the same level of impact, phenomena undifferentiated, undecipherable. Only the food that fed their hunger was real.

A key to believability is making readers believe that a character acts in a realistic way. In the chart below, note characteristics of Hattie and Dumile with a quotation that illustrates the characteristic.

Character Representation	Quote
Hattie: open to improving racial equality	"friendly lift of the eyebrow"
Dumile: hesitant but somewhat confident	"nervous white of his eyes"

41

●◆A second way to think about the believability is to look at the ending. Does the ending seem too easy? Too dramatic? Describe how believable you find the story's ending. Refer to specifics to illustrate your opinion.

Consider the believability of characters by examining their actions, their characteristics, and the ending of the story.

Three

Writing Unwritten Scenes

The writer is responsible for making a story believable, but the reader has a role as well. Readers may find themselves justifying a character's action, imagining the thoughts of characters, or filling in details of a character's history. Writing these unwritten scenes is a way of making the story believable.

●❖ Write an unwritten scene for "Comrades." You might write from the perspective of one of the young men, tell a related story about Hattie or Dumile, or create a new ending. Think of your unwritten scene as one that could be attached to the end of the story or inserted within the present story. Use Gordimer's style so that a reader would have a hard time knowing where Gordimer's writing ended and yours began.

42

By writing unwritten scenes, readers fill in missing perspectives, provide background information, or create a version of events to better understand the situation.

Four
Believing the Fantastic

With exotic **settings** and fantastic adventures, the fantasy story may be closer to our dreams than to our daily lives. What is the appeal of such tales, and how do they affect us? In some ways the believability is based on our capacity to wonder and imagine if life were different than it is. The following story from Salman Rushdie's novel *Haroun and the Sea of Stories* is a fantasy. Here the common, familiar experiences of human life are ignored or disregarded, but the events remind us somehow of the real world.

from "An Iff and a Butt" from *Haroun and the Sea of Stories*
by Salman Rushdie

So Iff the Water Genie told Haroun about the Ocean of the Streams of Story, and even though he was full of a sense of hopelessness and failure the magic of the Ocean began to have an effect on Haroun. He looked into the water and saw that it was made up of a thousand thousand thousand and one different currents, each one a different colour, weaving in and out of one another like a liquid tapestry of breathtaking complexity; and Iff explained that these were the Streams of Story, that each coloured strand represented and contained a single tale. Different parts of the Ocean contained different sorts of stories, and as all the stories that had ever been told and many that were still in the process of being invented could be found here, the Ocean of the Streams of Story was in fact the biggest library in the universe. And because the stories were held here in fluid form, they retained the ability to change, to become new versions of themselves, to join up with the other stories and so become yet other stories; so that unlike a library of books, the Ocean of the Streams of Story was much more than a storeroom of yarns. It was not dead but alive.

"And if you are very, very careful, or very, very highly skilled, you can dip a cup into the Ocean," Iff told Haroun, "like so," and here he produced a little golden cup from another of his waistcoat pockets, "and you can fill it with water from a single, pure Stream of Story, like so," as he did precisely that, "and then you can offer it to a young fellow who's feeling blue, so that the magic of the story can restore his spirits. Go on now; knock it back, have a swig, do yourself a favour," Iff concluded. "Guaranteed to make you feel A-number-one."

Haroun, without saying a word, took the golden cup and drank.

****

He found himself standing in a landscape that looked exactly like a giant chessboard. On every black square there was a monster: there were two-tongued snakes and lions with three rows of teeth, and four-headed dogs and five-headed demon kings and so on. He was, so to speak, looking out through the eyes of the young hero of the story. It was like being in the passenger seat of an automobile; all he had to do was watch, while the hero dispatched one monster after another and advanced up the chessboard towards the white stone tower at the end. At the top of the tower was (what else but) a single window, out of which there gazed (what else but) a captive princess. What Haroun

← *Response notes* →

43

from "An Iff and a Butt" from *Haroun and the Sea of Stories*
by Salman Rushdie

was experiencing, though he didn't know it, was Princess Rescue Story Number S/1001/ZHT/420/41(r)xi; and because the princess in this particular story had recently had a haircut and therefore had no long tresses to let down (unlike the heroine of Princess Rescue Story G/1001/RIM/777/M(w)i, better known as "Rapunzel"), Haroun as the hero was required to climb up the outside of the tower by clinging to the cracks between the stones with his bare hands and feet.

He was halfway up the tower when he noticed one of his hands beginning to change, becoming hairy, losing its human shape. Then his arms burst out of his shirt, and they too had grown hairy, and impossibly long, and had joints in the wrong places. He looked down and saw the same thing happening to his legs. When new limbs began to push themselves out from his sides, he understood that he was somehow turning into a monster just like those he had been killing; and above him the princess caught at her throat and cried out in a faint voice:

"Eek, my dearest, you have into a large spider turned."

As a spider he was able to make rapid progress to the top of the tower; but when he reached the window the princess produced a large kitchen knife and began to hack and saw at his limbs, crying rhythmically. *"Get* away spider, *go* back home," and he felt his grip on the stones of the tower grow looser; and then she managed to chop right through the arm nearest her, and he fell.

****

"Wake up, snap out of it, let's have you," he heard Iff anxiously calling. He opened his eyes to find himself lying full-length on the back of Butt the Hoopoe. Iff was sitting beside him, looking extremely worried and more than a little disappointed that Haroun had somehow managed to keep a firm grip on the Disconnecting Tool.

"What happened?" Iff asked. "You saved the princess and walked off into the sunset as specified, I presume? But then why all this moaning and groaning and turning and churning? Don't you *like* Princess Rescue Stories?"

Haroun recounted what had happened to him in the story, and both Iff and Butt became very serious indeed. "I can't believe it," Iff finally said. "It's a definite first, without parallel, never in all my born days."

"I'm almost glad to hear it," said Haroun. "Because I was thinking, that wasn't the *most* brilliant way to cheer me up."

"It's pollution," said the Water Genie gravely. "Don't you understand? Something, or somebody, has been putting filth into the Ocean. And obviously if filth gets into the stories, they go wrong. —Hoopoe, I've been away on my rounds too long. If there are traces of this pollution right up here in the Deep North, things at Gup City must be close to crisis. Quick, quick! Top speed ahead! This could mean war."

"War with whom?" Haroun wanted to know.

Iff and Butt shivered with something very like fear.

44

from "An Iff and a Butt" from *Haroun and the Sea of Stories*
by Salman Rushdie

"With the Land of Chup, on the Dark Side of Kahani," Butt the
Hoopoe answered without moving its beak. "This looks like the doing
of the leader of the Chupwalas, the Cultmaster of Bezaban."

"And who's that?" Haroun persevered, beginning to wish he'd
stayed in his peacock bed instead of getting muddled up with Water
Genies and Disconnecting Tools and talking mechanical Hoopoes and
story-oceans in the sky.

"His name," whispered the Water Genie, and the sky darkened for
an instant as he spoke it, "is Khattam-Shud."

Far away on the horizon, forked lightning glittered, once. Haroun
felt his blood run cold.

← Response notes →

Rushdie invites you into another world—a place where familiar stories get
twisted. How does he help you believe in certain facts about the fantasy world? The
passages below introduce something that you need to believe if you accept this
fantasy world.

●◆ Read each passage and list the fact or facts that you are asked to believe. Then
describe why these "facts" must be accepted if the story is to be believable.

" . . . and Iff explained that these were the Streams of Story, that each coloured
strand represented and contained a single tale. Different parts of the Ocean
contained different sorts of stories, and as all the stories that had ever been
told and many that were still in the process of being invented could be found
here, the Ocean of the Streams of Story was in fact the biggest library in the
universe."

45

". . . 'and you can fill it with water from a single, pure Stream of Story, like so,' as
he did precisely that, 'and then you can offer it to a young fellow who's feeling blue,
so that the magic of the story can restore his spirits. . . .' "

"What Haroun was experiencing, though he didn't know it, was Princess Rescue Story Number S/1001/ZHT/420/41(r)xi; and because the princess in this particular story had recently had a haircut and therefore had no long tresses to let down (unlike the heroine of Princess Rescue Story G/1001/RIM/777/M(w)i, better known as 'Rapunzel'), Haroun as the hero was required to climb up the outside of the tower by clinging to the cracks between the stones with his bare hands and feet."

●◆Find another passage that introduces one of the facts you are asked to believe and explain why it is important to the story.

quotation:

explanation:

A story with fantastic elements creates its own "facts" that push the reader to suspend disbelief and enter the world created by the writer.

Work with a partner to identify examples of where the more fantastical elements of the story are supported by realistic details. Discuss how the two work together to help you believe in this fantasy.

Five

Creating a Believable Fantasy

Part of what we learn from Iff the Water Genie is that in the Ocean of the Streams of Story there are "a thousand thousand thousand and one different currents, each with a different colour, weaving in and out of one another like a liquid tapestry of breathtaking complexity." But the Ocean has been polluted. What happens if "the richest," "the fairest," "the wisest," and "the cruelest" get all mixed up? Possibly Cinderella ends up in a deep sleep for a thousand years while Sleeping Beauty finds the glass slipper. One of the problems with polluted stories is that the reader has certain expectations about what will happen. The writer has a more difficult challenge in creating believability because the reader expects the story to go in a certain way. Try your hand at creating a polluted story.

●◆Choose two fairy tales that you know well—for example, Red Riding Hood, Cinderella, or Jack and the Beanstalk—and list what you remember about each one below.

Fairy Tale 1:

Fairy Tale 2:

47

●◆ Now, write the two stories into one fantasy that creates a "polluted" version similar to the blending of Haroun and Rapunzel in Rushdie's story. The pollution is intended to achieve some new meaning beyond what each story can tell separately.

Sometimes writers break readers' expectations of how a story gets told. Instead they create a different type of believability that will engage the readers' imaginations.

49

Seeing the World

Think back to the stories you read when you were a child. Did they take you to distant lands or times? Did you ride in spaceships to Mars or float down a river where danger lurked on either side? Literature is full of stories of adventure and the romance of travel —some true and some imaginary.

In some ways, reading is traveling. Through the words on the page, you can go anywhere. When you read literature about unfamiliar places and people, you have to stretch your imagination to see what the author is writing about. You need to pay attention to the writer's selection and use of details. You also must be alert to the writer's attitude toward the subject and his or her involvement in it. Then you know how to interpret the writer's impressions.

Active readers use their critical and imaginative skills to envision and understand every scene.

When you traveled somewhere new, did you ever have to make sense of an unfamiliar sight? What did you do? Perhaps you asked someone what it was or how it worked. Perhaps you read about it in a guidebook. Readers, too, have to make sense of the unfamiliar. Think about how you make sense of words and images that are unusual to you as you read an excerpt from "Subterranean Gothic." Note the way in which British travel writer Paul Theroux supplements his impressions of the New York subway with information from a variety of sources.

from **"Subterranean Gothic"** by Paul Theroux

← Response notes →

New Yorkers say some terrible things about the subway—that they hate it, or are scared stiff of it, or that it deserves to go broke. For tourists, it seems just another dangerous aspect of New York, though most don't know it exists. "I haven't been down there in years," is a common enough remark from a city dweller. Even people who ride it seem to agree that there is more Original Sin among subway passengers. And more desperation, too, making you think of choruses of "O dark dark dark. They all go into the dark . . . ."

"Subway" is not its name because, strictly-speaking, more than half of it is elevated. But which person who has ridden it lately is going to call it by its right name, "The Rapid Transit"? It is also frightful-looking. It has paint and signatures all over its aged face. The graffiti is bad, violent and destructive, and is so extensive and so dreadful it is hard to believe that the perpetrators are not the recipients of some enormous foundation grant. The subway has been vandalized from end to end. It smells so hideous you want to put a clothes-pin on your nose, and it is so noisy the sound actually hurts. Is it dangerous? Ask anyone and he or she will tell you there are about two murders a day on the subway. It really is the pits, people say.

You have to ride it for a while to find out what it is and who takes it and who gets killed on it.

It is full of surprises. Three and a half million fares a day pass through it, and in the first nine months of last year the total number of murder victims on the subway amounted to six. This half-dozen does not include suicides (one a week), "man-under" incidents (one a day), or "space-cases"—people who get themselves jammed between the train and the platform. Certainly the subway is very ugly and extremely noisy, but it only *looks* like a death-trap. People ride it looking stunned and holding their breath. It's not at all like the BART system in San Francisco, where people are constantly chattering, saying, "I'm going to my father's wedding," or "I'm looking after my mom's children," or "I've got a date with my fiancée's boyfriend." In New York, the subway is a serious matter—the rackety train, the silent passengers, the occasional scream.

Consider the sources that Theroux needed to write this piece. Mark the places in the text where he:

1. uses sensory details (sight, smell, sound, feel, taste)
2. refers to what others have told him
3. includes statistics

One additional source of information is the writer's impressions. It is important to read critically to find out the author's attitude toward the subject. Theroux includes details that seem odd to him and comments that reveal his attitude. Reread the passage and comment on the impression created by the following details.

Odd detail or comment	Impression created
". . . there is more Original Sin among subway passengers."	
". . . it is hard to believe that the perpetrators are not the recipients of some enormous foundation grant."	
the three comments that might be overheard on BART	

What hints are there about Theroux's attitude toward Americans? Summarize his impressions below.

Consider
the sources of information, including the author's attitude toward the subject, when reading descriptions of an unfamiliar subject.

The author's inner **conflicts** can also reveal his attitude toward a subject. In "Sea-Room," Jonathan Raban explains his desire to escape to the sea. At one time or another, almost everyone dreams of escaping. Run away to join the circus. Catch a ship and sail around the world. What inner conflicts compel people to escape?

from *"Sea-Room"* by Jonathan Raban

← Response notes →

Whenever I find myself growing grim about the mouth; whenever it is damp, drizzly November in my soul; whenever I find myself involuntarily pausing before coffin warehouses, and bringing up the rear of every funeral I meet; and especially whenever my hypos get such an upper hand of me, that it requires a strong moral principle to prevent me from deliberately stepping into the street, and methodically knocking people's hats off—then, I account it high time to get to sea as soon as I can. This is my substitute for pistol and ball. With a philosophical flourish Cato throws himself upon his sword; I quietly take to the ship.

—Herman Melville, *Moby Dick*

It was the classic last resort. I wanted to run away to sea.

It started as a nervous itch, like an attack of eczema. All spring and summer I scratched at it, and the more I scratched the more the affliction spread. There was no getting rid of the thing. Lodged in my head was an image, in suspiciously heightened colour, of a very small ship at sea.

It was more ark than boat. It contained the entire life of one man, and it floated serenely offshore: half in, half out of the world. The face of its solitary navigator was as dark as demerara. He wasn't flying a flag. His boat was a private empire, a sovereign state in miniature, a tight little, right little liberal regime. He was a world away from where I stood. Lucky man. He'd slung his hook, and upped and gone. Afloat, abroad, following his compass-needle as it trembled in its dish of paraffin, he was a figure of pure liberty. He had the world just where he wanted it. When he looked back at the land from which he'd sailed, it was arranged for him in brilliant perspective, its outlines clean, like the cut-out scenery of a toy theatre.

I was plagued by this character. Each time I gave him notice to quit my private territorial waters, he sailed mockingly past. Smoke from his pipe rose in a fine column of question marks over my horizon. His laughter was loud and derisive. He wouldn't go away.

I was landlocked and fidgety. I paced the deck of an urban flat and dreamed of sea-room, with the uncomfortable feeling that I'd picked up a dream which didn't belong to me, as if I'd tuned in my mental radio to the wrong station.

52

●◆ Take a few minutes to think about and explain how the narrator differs from the "solitary navigator" he envisions. List relevant details to support the differences you identify. Then continue reading.

....

....

....

....

....

←— Response notes —→

Lots of people would claim the dream as their own. The idea of taking ship and heading off into the blue is, after all, a central part of the mythology of being English. Elias Canetti writes that the "famous individualism" of the Englishman stems directly from his habit of thinking of himself as a lone mariner; a perception endorsed by whole libraries of bad Victorian novels.

In the books, the English are always running away to sea. The ocean is the natural refuge of every bankrupt, every young man crossed in love, every compromised second son. The Peregrines and Septimuses of the world behave like lemmings: their authors seem powerless to stop them from racing for the nearest quayside at the first sign of trouble.

They do it with such stylish finality too. The bag is secretly packed in the small hours, the farewell letter left like a suicide note beside the ormolu clock on the hall table. Goodbye, family! Goodbye, friends! Goodbye, England!

They close the front door behind them as gently as if they were dismantling a bomb. They tiptoe across the drive, careful not to wake the dogs, their faces grave at the audacity of what they've done. They pass the misty church, the doctor's house behind its cliff of pines, the bulky shadows of Home Farm. By sunrise, they're on the open road, their past already out of sight.

When next heard of, they are up on deck with a full gale blowing out of the Sou'west. The ship is falling away from under their feet in a mountainous swell. They cling to the shrouds, their hands bloody from hauling on ropes and scrubbing decks with holystone. They are changed men.

The sea voyage is more than an adventure; it is a rite of passage, as decisive as a wedding. It marks the end of the old self and the birth of the new. It is a great purifying ordeal. Storms and saltwater cleanse the ne'er-do-well and turn him into a hero. In the last chapter he will get the girl, the vicar's blessing and the family fortune.

I knew that I was pushing my luck, and running against the clock. Peregrine and Septimus aren't usually men of forty with dental

←—Response notes —→

problems and mortgages to pay. I wasn't a scapegrace young tough. I wasn't made for the outdoors. My experience of the sea was confined to paddling in it with the bottoms of my trousers rolled up, collecting coloured pebbles, and lolling on the edge of the ocean in a stripey deckchair until the peeling skin on my nose made me head back to the more manageable world of the hotel bar.

My kinship with the runaways was of a different kind. What I envied in them was the writing of their letters of farewell.

Dear Father,

By the time you read this, I shall be . . .

Magic words. I was excited by their gunpowdery whiff of action and decision. Both were in pretty short supply where I was sitting. Moping at my worktable, I decided to change a comma to a semicolon. Framed in the window under a bleary sky, the huge grey tub of the Kensal Green gasometer sank lugubriously downwards as West London cooked its Sunday lunch.

. . . far away on the high seas. Please tell Mother . . .

Well, I had fallen out with the family, too. I couldn't put a date on the quarrel: there'd been no firelit showdown in the library, no sign of the riding whip, not even any duns at the front door. It had been a long unloving wrangle, full of edgy silences, niggling resentments and strained efforts at politeness. One day I woke to realize that there was nowhere I felt less at home than home.

There is little physical action in this essay, but there is movement. It arises from tensions and conflicts. Go back to the text and mark the sections where Raban:

1. talks about his desire to go to sea

2. discusses the typical English travel pattern

3. talks about his reasons for wanting to leave

●◆Describe the tensions and conflict in Raban's life. How do they help explain his desire to leave home?

Movement in an essay can come from the author's inner tensions and conflicts. Watch for descriptions of differences between the writer and his dreams.

Three

Real and Imaginary Details

In some travel writing, the author is on a journey to learn about himself or herself. As a reader, you can expect to find at least two kinds of details in such writing. There will be physical details to describe actual people, objects, and places. There will also be imaginative details to describe what the writer hopes to find on the journey. In the excerpt below, Jonathan Raban, still dissatisfied with his life, looks for a boat to take him to sea.

from *"Sea-Room"* by Jonathan Raban

An hour or so before the house began to shudder to the cannonball passage of the underground trains, before the early-morning rattle of milk bottles on steps, I was woken by the bell of the convent down the road. It was ringing for Prime and sounded thin and squeaky like a wheezing lung. The sun never rises on North Kensington with any marked enthusiasm, and the light that had begun to smear the walls of the room looked dingy and secondhand. I didn't much care for the appearance of this new day, and took flight into a deep sea-dream.

In novels, when the black sheep of the family takes ship, his running away is really a means of coming home. His voyage restores him to his relations and to society. I had the same end in view. I wanted to go home; and the most direct, most exhilarating route back there lay by sea. Afloat with charts and compass, I'd find my bearings again. I saw myself inching along the coast, navigating my way around my own country and my own past, taking sights and soundings until I had the place's measure. It was to be an escape, an apprenticeship and a homecoming.

It was a consoling fantasy. I sustained it by going off at weekends and looking at real boats. As a minor consequence of the recession, every harbour in England was crowded with boats for sale: hulks under tarpaulins, rich men's toy motor cruisers, abandoned racing yachts, converted lifeboats and ships' tenders. Their prices were drifting steadily downwards, like the pound; and their brokers had the air of distressed gentlefolk eking out the last of the family capital. They made a feeble play of busyness and spotted me at once as another optimist trying to rid himself of his unaffordable boat. *No dice*, their eyes said, as they shuffled the paper on their desks.

"I'm looking for a boat to sail round Britain in," I said, trying the words out in the air to see if they had the ring of true idiocy.

"Ah. *Are* you now—" The broker's face was rearranging itself fast, but it looked as if he'd forgotten the expression of avuncular confidence that he was now trying to achieve. All his features stopped in mid-shift: they registered simple disbelief.

He showed me a wreck with a sprung plank. "She's just the job, old boy. It's what she was built for."

A sheet of flapping polythene had been pinned down over the foredeck to stop leaks. The glass was missing from a wheelhouse window. It was easy to see oneself going down to the bottom in a boat

← *Response notes:* →

55

like that. It had the strong aura of emergency flares, Mayday calls and strings of big bubbles.

"Know what she was up for when she first came in? Ten grand. And that was over four years ago—think what inflation must have done to that by now." The broker consulted the sky piously, as if the heavens were in the charge of a white-bearded wrathful old economist. "At two-five, old boy . . . two-five . . . she's a steal."

Lowering myself down slippery dockside ladders to inspect these unloved and unlovable craft, I felt safe enough. The voyage stayed securely in the realm of daydream. I liked the pretence involved in my seaside shopping expeditions, and from each broker I learned a new trick or two. I copied the way they dug their thumbnails into baulks of timber and the knowledgeable sniff with which they tasted the trapped air of the saloon. I picked up enough snippets of shoptalk to be able to speak menacingly of rubbing-strakes and keel-bolts; and soon the daydream itself began to be fleshed out in glibly realistic detail.

As I came to put names to all its parts, the boat in my head grew more substantial and particular by the day. Built to sail out of the confused seas of Ladbroke Grove and Notting Hill, it had to be tubby and trawler-like. It would be broad in the beam, high in the bow, and framed in oak. It would ride out dirty weather with the buoyancy of a puffin; inside, it would be as snug as a low-ceilinged tudor cottage. It was perfectly designed to go on imaginary voyages and make dream-landfalls.

Raban is telling two stories here. He is dreaming of the boat that will take him away from his current life and he is looking at real boats. Sort out the realistic physical details from the imaginary ones by filling in the chart.

Features of real boats	Features of imaginary boat
"a wreck with a sprung plank"	would have "the buoyancy of a puffin"

Pay attention to both the realistic and imaginary details in a travel text. They will give you clues about how the writer sees himself and his journey.

Four Point of View

Evelyn Waugh was an astute, witty observer of people. In his **satires**, he cheerfully pointed out their weaknesses and foibles. As you read Waugh's observations of a group of American tourists, note the ways that his **point of view** colors his description of the subject.

"American Tourists in Egypt" from *Labels: A Mediterranean Journey*
by Evolyn Waugh

←—— Response notes ——→

One day I went alone to Sakkara, the enormous necropolis some way down the Nile from Mena. There are two pyramids there, and a number of tombs; one of them, named unpronounceably the Mastaba of Ptahhotep, is exquisitely decorated in low relief. Another still more beautifully sculptured chamber is called more simply the Mastaba of Ti. As I emerged from this vault I came upon a large party of twenty or thirty indomitable Americans dragging their feet, under the leadership of a dragoman, across the sand from a charabanc. I fell in behind this party and followed them underground again, this time into a vast subterranean tunnel called the Serapeum, which, the guide explained, was the burial place of the sacred bulls. It was like a completely unilluminated tube-railway station. We were each given a candle, and our guide marched on in front with a magnesium flare. Even so, the remote corners were left in impenetrable darkness. On either side of our path were ranged the vast granite sarcophagi; we marched very solemnly the full length of the tunnel, our guide counting the coffins aloud for us; there were twenty-four of them, each so massive that the excavating engineers could devise no means of removing them. Most of the Americans counted aloud with him.

One is supposed, I know, to think of the past on these occasions; to conjure up the ruined streets of Memphis and to see in one's mind's eye the sacred procession as it wound up the avenue of sphinxes, mourning the dead bull; perhaps even to give license to one's fancy and invent some personal romance about the lives of these garlanded hymn-singers, and to generalize sagely about the mutability of human achievement. But I think we can leave all that to Hollywood. For my own part I found the present spectacle infinitely stimulating. What a funny lot we looked, trooping along that obscure gallery! First the Arab with his blazing white ribbon of magnesium, and behind him, clutching their candles, like penitents in procession, this whole rag-tag and bobtail of self-improvement and uplift. Some had been bitten by mosquitoes and bore swollen, asymmetrical faces; many were footsore, and limped and stumbled as they went; one felt faint and was sniffing "salts"; one coughed with dust; another had her eyes inflamed by the sun; another wore his arm in a sling, injured in heaven knows what endeavor; every one of the party in some way or another was bruised and upbraided by the thundering surf of education. And still they plunged on. One, two, three, four . . . twenty-four dead bulls; not twenty-three or twenty-five. How could they remember twenty-four? Why, to be sure, it was the number of Aunt Mabel's bedroom at Luxor. "How did the bulls die?" one of them asks.

57

"American Tourists in Egypt" from *Labels: A Mediterranean Journey*
by Evelyn Waugh

← Response notes →

"What did he ask?" chatter the others.

"What did the guide answer?" they want to know.

"How *did* the bulls die?"

"How much did it cost?" asks another. "You can't build a place like this for nothing."

"We don't spend money that way nowadays."

"Fancy spending all that burying bulls . . ."

Oh, ladies and gentlemen, I longed to declaim, dear ladies and gentlemen, fancy crossing the Atlantic Ocean, fancy coming all this way in the heat, fancy enduring all these extremities of discomfort and exertion; fancy spending all this money, to see a hole in the sand where, three thousand years ago, a foreign race whose motives must forever remain inexplicable interred the carcasses of twenty-four bulls. Surely the laugh, dear ladies and gentlemen, is on us.

But I remembered I was a gate-crasher in this party and remained silent.

A **satire** develops through a series of contrasts, highlighting the discrepancies between the way things should be and the way they are. In this selection, Waugh is satirizing the American tourists. In the boxes, quote words and phrases from the text that support his purposes.

Purpose: show how insignificant the tourists are in relation to the monuments

"Sakkarra, the enormous necropolis" "this whole rag-tag and bobtail of self-improvement and uplift"

Purpose: contrast the sacred procession with the current "procession"

"'How much did it cost?'"

Writers of satire reveal through their point of view the weaknesses or flaws in human beings. When reading satire, it is important to pay attention to the contrasting details the writer uses.

Five

Establishing Points of Reference

Travel writing is about people as much as places. One challenge for the travel writer is to introduce people whose actions and customs may be unfamiliar. Isabel Fonseca had a special challenge in describing the Gypsies of Albania. The Gypsies distrust outsiders and often delight in telling stories to fool reporters. Fonseca combines what they say with what she observes in her book *Bury Me Standing*. In the following excerpt, she focuses on women's work.

from ***Bury Me Standing*** by Isabel Fonseca

←—Response notes—→

Twenty-five square feet of children, chickens, and clothes hanging out to dry: life for the Dukas took place in the courtyard. Especially the lives of the women. Apart from Jeta—and except for quick dashes for bread or butane for the outdoor cooking ring, and maybe, in the evening, a short after-work visit to a sister or friend in the quarter—the women were not allowed out. In any case they were too busy.

There are many sources of advice on how to be a good *bori*, such as this proverb from Slovakia: *Ajsi bori lachi: xal bilondo, phenel londo*—"Such a daughter-in-law is good who eats unsalted food and says it is salted." Modesty and submissiveness were essential, to be sure, but in the main these girls *worked*. From around five-thirty in the morning, the day was a cycle of duties, with the burden falling on Viollca and Mirella, the younger wives. These women were never called by their names, or "wife" (*romni*), or any term of endearment by their husbands; nor were they called "mother" (*daj*) by their children. Everyone referred to them as the *boria*—the brides, or daughters-in-law—and indeed it was Jeta to whom they were answerable, not to their menfolk. So, despite the institution of male laziness, this really was a matriarchy. Only Jeta could inspire fear. That the men did nothing came very quickly to seem not so much a privilege as a relegation to child status.

The girls ignored my daily request to be woken up. I kept trying to program or dream myself into their rhythm, but the body did not want to get up before the sun did (and I really couldn't set my alarm clock, and wake all the children, just to watch the girls work). One night though, I'd slept badly and was still trying to settle down when the *boria* stirred in the dark and began their day. Viollca and Mirella (called Lela) got up before everyone else, including Dritta and including the *khania*, the hens. They moved silently about the courtyard, collecting wood from the tidy pile that they maintained along one inner wall of the courtyard. In the sooty light, they built their neat fire, always the same, neither too high nor too feeble. They bailed water from an old oil drum into cans, which they arranged among the burning logs. There was fuel, but it was expensive, and so it was reserved for Jeta's cooking. The *boria* had to build their fires from scratch.

While the water heated up, the girls gathered any vaguely soiled blankets, rugs, and clothes for washing. Each had her own work station in a different corner of the courtyard and there set up her

59

long tin tub on an old wooden crate; then together they lifted each of the heavy slate washboards into the tubs. The tubs were thigh-high or lower, and so both girls scrubbed in a hunched, backbreaking position. My loudly whispered pleas to "bend from the knee" inspired an exchange of furtive, pitying giggles and glances.

Each broke off a hunk of soap from the Parmesan glacier in the storage cupboard and dropped it into her tub. (My own soap *bar* was an exotic item, regarded with skeptical wonder, as if it were a palm-top computer.) They poured in boiling water and swirled it around, beginning the real ritual: hours of trancelike, rhythmical rubbing, interrupted now by a stream of new demands—a hungry child, an insufficiently caffeinated father-in-law. And they really rubbed, with such vigor that they seemed to be trying to wring the color from every bit of soaking cloth. Washing—keeping clothes and houses and themselves clean—was the *boria's* most important job. They worked in a competitive spirit, especially once Dritta made her appearance. And all of them had to be in mind of what they were washing: men's clothes and women's clothes were to be scrubbed separately, as were children's. Another tub was reserved for the kids themselves and another for dishes and pots. They had correspondingly designated towels or rags, and never transferred a bit of tide-worn soap, always hacking off a new hunk for each new task.

60

●◆Explore the implications or meanings of the scene Fonseca describes. How does she combine details that are familiar and those that are unfamiliar to teach something about the way of life of the Gypsies?

Familiar action	Unfamiliar action	Meaning
washing clothes	getting up before dawn	the women work long hours
women do the washing	they are never referred to as wife or mother	

Establish your own points of reference when reading about unfamiliar subjects. Notice key details and make comparisons to what you do know.

Perspectives on a Subject: Finding a Home

To choose a college, would you just read the catalog? Probably not. You would check with people you know who have attended school there, read recommendations in guidebooks, and talk with your school counselor. You might visit the campus. The need to explore all of the angles is the same for reading about a subject. You can better understand what you read by exploring the many perspectives writers have taken on a subject.

The subject of home is complicated for British writers. There are many literary celebrations of the British Isles. One of the most famous is from Shakespeare's *Richard II*: "This blessed plot, this earth, this realm, this England."

Yet, there is no one definition of home for a British writer. Because of the British Empire, writers as diverse as Virginia Woolf and the West Indian Derek Walcott are part of the same tradition. What each calls home is very different—each provides a perspective on the idea of home.

When you read what writers say about finding a home, you will learn about the approaches authors use to develop a subject.

One
Idea Association

Writers often try to tap into their readers' associations with a topic. In this way, writers can reduce explanation and connect with readers' experiences. Before you read one writer's memory of her childhood home, record your own associations. Put the words "childhood home" in the center of the cluster and put related words and phrases on the spokes.

Now, read Jessica Mitford's memory of her home, Swinbrook, in the English countryside in the early part of the twentieth century.

from *Daughters and Rebels* by Jessica Mitford

←— Response notes —→

Growing up in the English countryside seemed an interminable process. Freezing winter gave way to frosty spring, which in turn merged into chilly summer—but nothing ever, ever happened. The lyrical, soft beauty of changing seasons in the Cotswolds literally left us cold. "Oh, to be in England Now that April's there," or, "Fair daffodils, we weep to see you haste away so soon . . ." The words were evocative enough, but I was not much of an April noticer or daffodil fancier. It never occurred to me to be happy with my lot. Knowing few children of my age with whom to compare notes, I envied the children of literature to whom interesting things were always happening: "Oliver Twist was so *lucky* to live in a fascinating orphanage!"

Nevertheless, there were occasional diversions. Sometimes we went up to London to stay at our mews in Rutland Gate for Christmas shopping (or shoplifting, depending on whether we were accompanied by Nanny or by Miss Bunting), and sometimes, when Swinbrook was let for a few months, a full-scale migration, Nanny, governess, maids, dogs, Enid, Miranda, dove and all of us, went to my mother's house on the outskirts of High Wycombe. But these small excursions only served to emphasize the dullness of life at Swinbrook.

We were as though caught in a timeproofed corner of the world, foster children, if not exactly of silence, at least of slow time. The very landscape, cluttered up with history, was disconcertingly filled with evidence of the changelessness of things. The main road to Oxford, built by Julius Caesar two thousand years ago, had been altered only by modern surfacing for the convenience of motorists; Roman coins, thrown up by the plow as though carelessly dropped only yesterday, were to be had for the gathering. As part of our lessons we kept Century Notebooks, a page for each century, in which we listed by date the main battles, reigns of kings and queens, scientific inventions. Human history seemed so depressingly short as one turned the pages. The French Revolution only two pages back, and flip! here we are at the twenty-first century, all of us dead and buried—but what will there be to show for it? "Precious little, if we're going to be stuck at Swinbrook for the rest of our lives," I mused sadly.

The great golden goal of every childhood—being a Grownup—seemed impossibly far away. There were for us no intermediate goals to fill the great, dull gap; no graduation from one stage of education to the next; no adolescent "first parties" to look forward to. You were a child, living within all the bounds and restrictions of childhood, from birth until you reached the age of seventeen or eighteen, depending on where your birthday fell in relation to the London season. Life broke down to an endless series of unconnected details, the days punctuated by lessons, meals and walks, the weeks by occasional visits from relations or the older children's friends, the months and years by the unexpected and unplanned for. . . .

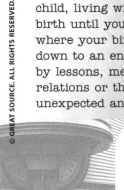

If Mitford had filled out a cluster as you did, what details would she have put in it? Underline the words or phrases in the text you think she would have listed. If there are additional words that you think she would have associated with "childhood home," put those in the response notes. How do Mitford's associations compare with yours? Circle the details on your cluster that are similar to hers.

●◆ Now, use your details to write a brief sketch of your childhood home. You may want to use Mitford's description as a model.

Authors develop a subject with ideas and details that readers can relate to.

Two

Defining a Subject Through Objects

The objects that people select can reveal aspects of their personality. In some cases, one's house is the most revealing of all. In an essay, Virginia Woolf described famous Englishmen through their houses. Below is her description of the house of the Scottish essayist and historian Thomas Carlyle. We often make distinctions between houses and homes, instilling homes with more emotional value and personality. Is Woolf making such a distinction?

from **"Great Men's Houses"** by Virginia Woolf

←—Response notes—→

London, happily, is becoming full of great men's houses, bought for the nation and preserved entire with the chairs they sat on and the cups they drank from, their umbrellas and their chests of drawers. And it is no frivolous curiosity that sends us to Dickens's house and Johnson's house and Carlyle's house and Keats's house. We know them from their houses—it would seem to be a fact that writers stamp themselves upon their possessions more indelibly than other people. Of artistic taste they may have none; but they seem always to possess a much rarer and more interesting gift—a faculty for housing themselves appropriately, for making the table, the chair, the curtain, the carpet into their own image.

Take the Carlyles, for instance. One hour spent in 5 Cheyne Row will tell us more about them and their lives than we can learn from all the biographies. Go down into the kitchen. There, in two seconds, one is made acquainted with a fact that escaped the attention of Froude, and yet was of incalculable importance—they had no water laid on. Every drop that the Carlyles used—and they were Scots, fanatical in their cleanliness—had to be pumped by hand from a well in the kitchen. There is the well at this moment and the pump and the stone trough into which the cold water trickled. And here, too, is the wide and wasteful old grate upon which all kettles had to be boiled if they wanted a hot bath; and here is the cracked yellow tin bath, so deep and so narrow, which had to be filled with the cans of hot water that the maid first pumped and then boiled and then carried up three flights of stairs from the basement.

The high old house without water, without electric light, without gas fires, full of books and coal smoke and four-poster beds and mahogany cupboards, where two of the most nervous and exacting people of their time lived, year in year out, was served by one unfortunate maid. All through the mid-Victorian age the house was necessarily a battlefield where daily, summer and winter, mistress and maid fought against dirt and cold for cleanliness and warmth. The stairs, carved as they are and wide and dignified, seem worn by the feet of harassed women carrying tin cans. The high panelled rooms seem to echo with the sound of pumping and the swish of scrubbing. The voice of the house—and all houses have voices—is the voice of pumping and scrubbing, of coughing and groaning. Up in the attic under a skylight Carlyle groaned, as he wrestled with his history, on

65

a horsehair chair, while a yellow shaft of London light fell upon his papers and the rattle of a barrel organ and the raucous shouts of street hawkers came through walls whose double thickness distorted but by no means excluded the sound. And the season of the house—for every house has its season—seems to be always the month of February, when cold and fog are in the street and torches flare and the rattle of wheels grows suddenly loud and dies away. February after February Mrs. Carlyle lay coughing in the large four-poster hung with maroon curtains in which she was born, and as she coughed the many problems of the incessant battle, against dirt, against cold, came before her. The horsehair couch needed recovering; the drawing-room paper with its small, dark pattern needed cleaning; the yellow varnish on the panels was cracked and peeling—all must be stitched, cleansed, scoured with her own hands; and had she, or had she not, demolished the bugs that bred and bred in the ancient wood panelling? So the long watches of the sleepless night passed, and then she heard Mr. Carlyle stir above her, and held her breath and wondered if Helen were up and had lit the fire and heated the water for his shaving. Another day had dawned and the pumping and the scrubbing must begin again.

Thus number 5 Cheyne Row is not so much a dwelling-place as a battlefield—the scene of labor, effort and perpetual struggle. Few of the spoils of life—its graces and its luxuries—survive to tell us that the battle was worth the effort. The relics of drawing-room and study are like the relics picked up on other battlefields. Here is a packet of old steel nibs; a broken clay pipe; a pen-holder such as schoolboys use; a few cups of white and gold china, much chipped; a horsehair sofa and a yellow tin bath. Here, too, is a cast of the thin worn hands that worked here; and of the excruciated and ravished face of Carlyle when his life was done and he lay dead here. Even the garden at the back of the house seems to be not a place of rest and recreation, but another smaller battlefield marked with a tombstone beneath which a dog lies buried. By pumping and by scrubbing, days of victory, evenings of peace and splendor were won, of course. Mrs. Carlyle sat, as we see from the picture, in a fine silk dress, in a chair pulled up to a blazing fire and had everything seemly and solid about her; but at what cost had she won it! Her cheeks are hollow; bitterness and suffering mingle in the half-tender, half-tortured expression of the eyes. Such is the effect of a pump in the basement and a yellow tin bath up three pairs of stairs. Both husband and wife had genius; they loved each other; but what can genius and love avail against bugs and tin baths and pumps in the basement?

It is impossible not to believe that half their quarrels might have been spared and their lives immeasurably sweetened if only number 5 Cheyne Row had possessed, as the house agents put it, bath, h. and c., gas fires in the bedrooms, all modern conveniences and indoor sanitation. But then, we reflect, as we cross the worn threshold, Carlyle with hot water laid on would not have been Carlyle; and Mrs. Carlyle without bugs to kill would have been a different woman from the one we know.

Woolf describes the house of the Carlyles as "a battlefield." Her direct descriptions are of the house, not its inhabitants, but you can infer characteristics of the Carlyles from the descriptions. Use the chart to show how descriptions of the house imply aspects of personality.

Description	Personality
"The high old house without water, without electric light, without gas fires. . ."	Home was not a place of comfort, but of work.

●◆ Write a brief description of your impression of the Carlyles based on Woolf's description of their house and the inferences you made.

67

> One way to develop a subject is to use objects that represent aspects of the subject.

Three

Developing Contrasts

Virginia Woolf used contrast to develop her essay about great men's houses. After describing the Carlyles, she turns to John Keats and offers a completely different impression of a "great man." John Keats and his friend Charles Brown shared a house in Hampstead next door to Keats' beloved, Fanny Brawne, and her mother.

from **"Great Men's Houses"** by Virginia Woolf

← *Response notes* →

An age seems to separate the house in Chelsea where the Carlyles lived from the house in Hampstead which was shared by Keats and Brown and the Brawnes. If houses have their voices and places their seasons, it is always spring in Hampstead as it is always February in Cheyne Row. By some miracle, too, Hampstead has always remained not a suburb or a piece of antiquity engulfed in the modern world, but a place with a character peculiar to itself. It is not a place where one makes money, or goes when one has money to spend. The signs of discreet retirement are stamped on it. Its houses are neat boxes such as front the sea at Brighton with bow windows and balconies and deck chairs on verandahs. It has style and intention as if designed for people of modest income and some leisure who seek rest and recreation. Its prevailing colors are the pale pinks and blues that seem to harmonize with the blue sea and the white sand; and yet there is an urbanity in the style which proclaims the neighborhood of a great city. Even in the twentieth century this serenity still pervades the suburb of Hampstead. Its bow windows still look out upon vales and trees and ponds and barking dogs and couples sauntering arm in arm and pausing, here on the hilltop, to look at the distant domes and pinnacles of London, as they sauntered and paused and looked when Keats lived here. For Keats lived up the lane in a little white house behind wooden palings. Nothing has been much changed since his day. But as we enter the house in which Keats lived some mournful shadow seems to fall across the garden. A tree has fallen and lies propped. Waving branches cast their shadows up and down over the flat white walls of the house. Here, for all the gaiety and serenity of the neighborhood, the nightingale sang; here, if anywhere, fever and anguish had their dwelling and paced this little green plot oppressed with the sense of quick-coming death and the shortness of life and the passion of love and its misery.

Yet if Keats left any impress upon his house it is the impression not of fever, but of that clarity and dignity which come from order and self-control. The rooms are small but shapely; downstairs the long windows are so large that half the wall seems made of light. Two chairs turned together are close to the window as if someone had sat there reading and had just got up and left the room. The figure of the reader must have been splashed with shade and sun as the hanging leaves stirred in the breeze. Birds must have hopped close to his foot. The room is empty save for the two chairs, for Keats had few possessions, little furniture and not more, he said, than one hundred

68

from **"Great Men's Houses"** by Virginia Woolf

and fifty books. And perhaps it is because the rooms are so empty and furnished rather with light and shadow than with chairs and tables that one does not think of people, here where so many people have lived. The imagination does not evoke scenes. It does not strike one that there must have been eating and drinking here; people must have come in and out; they must have put down bags, left parcels; they must have scrubbed and cleaned and done battle with dirt and disorder and carried cans of water from the basement to the bedrooms. All the traffic of life is silenced. The voice of the house is the voice of leaves brushing in the wind; of branches stirring in the garden. Only one presence—that of Keats himself—dwells here. And even he, though his picture is on every wall, seems to come silently, on the broad shafts of light, without body or footfall. Here he sat on the chair in the window and listened without moving, and saw without starting, and turned the page without haste though his time was so short.

There is an air of heroic equanimity about the house in spite of the death masks and the brittle yellow wreaths and the other grisly memorials which remind us that Keats died young and unknown and in exile. Life goes on outside the window. Behind this calm, this rustling of leaves, one hears the far-off rattle of wheels, the bark of dogs fetching and carrying sticks from the pond. Life goes on outside the wooden paling. When we shut the gate upon the grass and the tree where the nightingale sang we find, quite rightly, the butcher delivering his meat from a small red motor van at the house next door. If we cross the road, taking care not to be cut down by some rash driver—for they drive at a great pace down these wide streets— we shall find ourselves on top of the hill and beneath shall see the whole of London lying below us. It is a view of perpetual fascination at all hours and in all seasons. One sees London as a whole—London crowded and ribbed and compact, with its dominant domes, its guardian cathedrals; its chimneys and spires; its cranes and gasometers; and the perpetual smoke which no spring or autumn ever blows away. London has lain there time out of mind scarring that stretch of earth deeper and deeper, making it more uneasy, lumped and tumultuous, branding it for ever with an indelible scar. There it lies in layers, in strata, bristling and billowing with rolls of smoke always caught on its pinnacles. And yet from Parliament Hill one can see, too, the country beyond. There are hills on the further side in whose woods birds are singing, and some stoat or rabbit pauses, in dead silence, with paw lifted to listen intently to rustlings among the leaves. To look over London from this hill Keats came and Coleridge and Shakespeare, perhaps. And here at this very moment the usual young man sits on an iron bench clasping to his arms the usual young woman.

Woolf provides more than a description of houses in "Great Men's Houses." She also characterizes each house as having a "voice" and a "season." Many people would suggest that those are characteristics of a home. With a partner, discuss the similarities and contrasts between the houses of the two men and Woolf's idea of a "home."

•◆Using Woolf's techniques of selecting objects and finding contrasts, describe a dwelling that you know. Use details in your description that convey the mood and personality of the place.

70

Using contrasting details can highlight features of a topic more vividly than description alone.

Four

Changing Perspectives

The houses in Woolf's essay are definitely English. The location and the objects in them, as Woolf describes them, include details associated with England. The tea cups, the crowded streets of Chelsea, and the noises outside the windows all place the subjects of this essay in England.

But "finding a home" means something different to people whose countries were British colonies. Wole Soyinka, born in Nigeria, attended college in London in the 1950s. He wrote "Telephone Conversation" about one of his own experiences. Details such as "pillar-box" for mailbox and the "red booth" of a public telephone with two buttons, one for speaking and one for listening, set the scene in London.

Response notes

Telephone Conversation
Wole Soyinka

The price seemed reasonable, location
Indifferent. The landlady swore she lived
Off premises. Nothing remained
But self-confession. "Madam," I warned,
"I hate a wasted journey—I am African."
Silence. Silenced transmission of
Pressurized good-breeding. Voice, when it came,
Lipstick coated, long gold-rolled
Cigarette-holder pipped. Caught I was, foully.

"HOW DARK?" . . . I had not misheard. . . "ARE YOU LIGHT OR
VERY DARK?" Button B. Button A. Stench
Of rancid breath of public hide-and-speak.
Red booth. Red pillar-box. Red double-tiered
Omnibus squelching tar. It *was* real! Shamed
By ill-mannered silence, surrender
Pushed dumbfoundment to beg simplification.
Considerate she was, varying the emphasis—

"ARE YOU DARK? OR VERY LIGHT?" Revelation came.
"You mean—like plain or milk chocolate?"
Her assent was clinical, crushing in its light
Impersonality. Rapidly, wavelength adjusted,
I chose. "West African sepia"—and as an afterthought,
"Down in my passport." Silence for spectroscopic
Flight of fancy, till truthfulness clanged her accent
Hard on the mouthpiece. "WHAT'S THAT?" conceding,
"DON'T KNOW WHAT THAT IS." "Like brunette."

71

"THAT'S DARK, ISN'T IT?" "Not altogether.
Facially, I am brunette, but madam, you should see
The rest of me. Palm of my hand, soles of my feet
Are a peroxide blonde. Friction, caused—
Foolishly, madam—by sitting down, has turned
My bottom raven black—One moment madam!"—sensing
Her receiver rearing on the thunderclap
About my ears—"Madam," I pleaded, "wouldn't you rather
See for yourself?"

Response notes

●◆ Do you think the woman even heard his last words? If so, how do you think she replied? Write the continuation of this conversation, taking on the perspective of either the speaker in the poem or the British woman.

72

Shifting
perspectives on a subject
reveals aspects of it that might
otherwise be overlooked and enriches
the reader's understanding of
the topic.

Five
Irony and Double Meanings

When a writer wants readers to realize the shortcomings or flaws in a society, he or she may use **irony**. The contrast between what is said and what is really meant can reveal the discrepancy between an ideal and reality. Derek Walcott uses irony and words with double meanings in "The Virgins."

As you read the poem, consider how his life might have influenced what the speaker says. Walcott was born on St. Lucia, an island in the West Indies that was a British colony. In this poem, he writes about Frederiksted, a city on St. Croix, one of the U.S. Virgin Islands.

The Virgins
Derek Walcott

Down the dead streets of sun-stoned Frederiksted,
the first free port to die for tourism,
strolling at funeral pace, I am reminded
of life not lost to the American dream;
but my small-islander's simplicities
can't better our new empire's civilized
exchange of cameras, watches, perfumes, brandies
for the good life, so cheaply underpriced
that only the crime rate is on the rise
in streets blighted with sun, stone arches
and plazas blown dry by the hysteria
of rumor. A condominium drowns
in vacancy; its bargains are dusted,
but only a jeweled housefly drones
over the bargains. The roulettes spin
rustily to the wind—the vigorous trade
that every morning would begin afresh
by revving up green water around the pierhead
heading for where the banks of silver thresh.

Response notes

The speaker is clearly not happy about what has happened to his home. How does Walcott use irony and words with double meanings to show that unhappiness? Reread the poem, using this code to mark his techniques:

I for ironic statement

N for words with negative connotations, such as *blighted*

D for words with double meanings such as *trade* that could mean trade winds or commerce

Discuss with a partner some of the double meanings in this poem. Record your findings in the chart on the next page.

Word	Meanings
die	1.
	2.
vigorous trade	1.
	2.
banks of silver	1.
	2.

●◆ Use Walcott's poem as a model for a poem or paragraph of your own, describing a real or imagined change to your home. Consider whether or not the change is for the better. Use irony and double meanings to show the discrepancy between the ideal and the real.

_____

_____

_____

_____

74

_____

_____

_____

_____

_____

_____

_____

_____

_____

_____

_____

_____

Writers may use irony and words with double meanings to show the discrepancies between the ideal and the real forms of a subject.

Writing from Models

The goal of modeling is to help you become a discerning reader and perceptive writer. Many writers have talked about how, during their formative years, they either consciously or unconsciously imitated other writers whom they admired. Perhaps you can think of someone whose style you would like to imitate.

Writing from models requires close reading. It mirrors the way your mind works and lets you get inside the author's head. As you work with a piece of literature, you imitate the author's intent, point of view, and sentence structure. At the same time, you practice ways of writing that will give you additional options in creating your own structure and style.

The first reading of a poem should be without preconceptions and, as much as possible, without expectations. If the author is one we already know, we tend to approach a new poem with some expectations, but even then we may be surprised. Read "Hawk Roosting" with your eyes and mind open.

Response notes

Hawk Roosting
Ted Hughes

I sit in the top of the wood, my eyes closed.
Inaction, no falsifying dream
Between my hooked head and hooked feet:
Or in sleep rehearse perfect kills and eat.

The convenience of the high trees!
The air's buoyancy and the sun's ray
Are of advantage to me;
And the earth's face upward for my inspection.

My feet are locked upon the rough bark.
It took the whole of Creation
To produce my foot, my each feather:
Now I hold Creation in my foot

Or fly up, and revolve it all slowly—
I kill where I please because it is all mine.
There is no sophistry in my body:
My manners are tearing off heads—

The allotment of death.
For the one path of my flight is direct
Through the bones of the living.
No arguments assert my right:

The sun is behind me.
Nothing has changed since I began.
My eye has permitted no change.
I am going to keep things like this.

76

Discuss the following questions with a partner. Then write a summary of your responses:

- What words or phrases stopped you as you read, and perhaps puzzled you?
- How does the pattern of the poem—the **rhyming** lines, the **rhythmic** four-line stanzas—fit with the character of the hawk as Hughes presents it?
- How effective was Ted Hughes in putting you inside the mind of the hawk?
- In what way, if any, did the poem change what you think about hawks?

Select an animal that you can write knowledgeably about. Jot down or cluster what you know about its habits, its way of life, and so on. Then make some notes about what it would be like to be in the mind of this animal, looking out from its eyes. How does the world look from behind its eyes?

77

●❖ Reread Ted Hughes's poem and your notes. Then construct a poem in which the speaker is the animal you have chosen. Pay careful attention to the point of view. Write three or more four-line stanzas. Notice that there are no excess words in "Hawk Roosting," so make every word in your poem count.

Understanding a poem through modeling provides insight into points of view other than your own.

Two
Spinoff Modeling

Read this poem by Stephen Spender first for what it says. Then reread, making notes about what thoughts it triggered for you. Note lines that you like, phrases that you find evocative, and your questions.

I Think Continually of Those
Stephen Spender

I think continually of those who were truly great.
Who, from the womb, remembered the soul's history
Through corridors of light where the hours are suns,
Endless and singing. Whose lovely ambition
Was that their lips, still touched with fire,
Should tell of the spirit clothed from head to foot in song.
And who hoarded from the spring branches
The desires falling across their bodies like blossoms.

What is precious is never to forget
The essential delight of the blood drawn from ageless springs
Breaking through rocks in worlds before our earth.
Never to deny its pleasure in the morning simple light
Nor its grave evening demand for love.
Never to allow gradually the traffic to smother
With noise and fog the flowering of the spirit.

Near the snow, near the sun, in the highest fields
See how these names are fêted by the waving grass,
And by the streamers of white cloud,
And whispers of wind in the listening sky.
The names of those who in their lives fought for life,
Who wore at their hearts the fire's center.
Born of the sun they traveled a short while towards the sun,
And left the vivid air signed with their honor.

Response notes

79

●◆ Whose names come to mind after reading this poem? Write down the names of people who, in your opinion, were "truly great."

●◆ Write a poem beginning "I think continually of those who were truly great."
Then intermix your own lines and Spender's in two or three stanzas. You might
begin your second stanza "What is precious is never to forget. . . ." Since this is a
practice spinoff poem, use as much or as little of Spender's poem as you need.
Beneath the title of your poem, write "after Stephen Spender" as a way of
acknowledging the inspiration for your model.

Poets
often spin off a poem from
the inspiration of another poet's
lines. It is a method of practice
and interpretation.

Modeling an Ode

Odes are poems that are directly addressed to a subject. They range from very serious poems written as memorials to lighthearted poems addressed to what we might consider trivial subjects. There is an ode by Robert Burns entitled "To a Louse." Below is a serious ode by A. E. Housman.

To an Athlete Dying Young
A. E. Housman

Response notes

The time you won your town the race
We chaired you through the market-place;
Man and boy stood cheering by,
And home we brought you shoulder-high.

Today, the road all runners come,
Shoulder-high we bring you home,
And set you at your threshold down,
Townsman of a stiller town.

Smart lad, to slip betimes away
From fields where glory does not stay,
And early though the laurel grows
It withers quicker than the rose.

Eyes the shady night has shut
Cannot see the record cut,
And silence sounds no worse than cheers
After earth has stopped the ears.

Now you will not swell the rout
Of lads that wore their honors out,
Runners whom renown outran
And the name died before the man.

So set, before its echoes fade,
The fleet foot on the sill of shade,
And hold to the low lintel up
The still-defended challenge-cup.

And round that early-laureled head
Will flock to gaze the strengthless dead,
And find unwithered on its curls
The garland briefer than a girl's.

81

Like many **odes**, this one is written in a classical style. Notice the regular pattern of **rhythm** and **rhyme**. Notice also that Housman sometimes inverts the natural word order. ("The time you won your town the race" should be, "The time you won the race for your town.") This technique is very common in older verse.

●◆Often, it is useful to paraphrase a poem. Try to summarize what Housman is saying in "To an Athlete Dying Young" in one sentence.

●◆Now try your hand at writing an ode. Your subject can be serious or trivial. For this model, try keeping to a strict rhythm (four **feet** to a line) and rhyme scheme (rhyming **couplets**). (For explanations of rhythm and rhyme, see pages 215–218.) Address your poem directly to the subject.

The ode is a classical form still widely used by poets for both serious and trivial subjects.

Four Modeling Voice

Read Henry Reed's "Naming of Parts," listening for the way the two voices in the poem alternate and merge.

"Naming of Parts" from *Lessons of the War*
Henry Reed

Today we have naming of parts. Yesterday,
We had daily cleaning. And tomorrow morning,
We shall have what to do after firing. But today,
Today we have naming of parts. Japonica
Glistens like coral in all of the neighboring gardens,
        And today we have naming of parts.

This is the lower sling swivel. And this
Is the upper sling swivel, whose use you will see,
When you are given your slings. And this is the piling swivel,
Which in your case you have not got. The branches
Hold in the gardens their silent, eloquent gestures,
        Which in our case we have not got.

This is the safety-catch, which is always released
With an easy flick of the thumb. And please do not let me
See anyone using his finger. You can do it quite easy
If you have any strength in your thumb. The blossoms
Are fragile and motionless, never letting anyone see
        Any of them using their finger.

And this you can see is the bolt. The purpose of this
Is to open the breech, as you see. We can slide it
Rapidly backwards and forwards: we call this
Easing the spring. And rapidly backwards and forwards
The early bees are assaulting and fumbling the flowers:
        They call it easing the Spring.

They call it easing the Spring: it is perfectly easy
If you have any strength in your thumb: like the bolt,
And the breech, and the cocking-piece, and the point of balance,
Which in our case we have not got; and the almond-blossom
Silent in all of the gardens and the bees going backwards and forwards,
        For today we have naming of parts.

Response notes

Reread the poem with an ear toward identifying the two voices of the narrator. Use parentheses to identify the inner reflective voice that shows what the narrator is thinking.

Underline or highlight any lines that are ambiguous—that apply both to the events of the military inspection and also to the narrator's inner reflections. Look, for example, at the line "They call it easing the Spring." (Notice the double meaning of *spring*.)

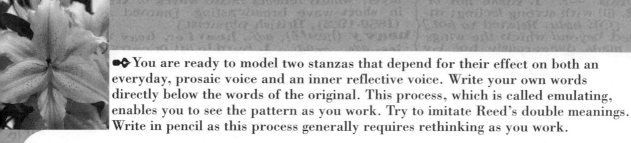

➦ You are ready to model two stanzas that depend for their effect on both an everyday, prosaic voice and an inner reflective voice. Write your own words directly below the words of the original. This process, which is called emulating, enables you to see the pattern as you work. Try to imitate Reed's double meanings. Write in pencil as this process generally requires rethinking as you work.

And this you can see is the bolt. The purpose of this

....

Is to open the breech, as you see. We can slide it

....

Rapidly backwards and forwards: we call this

....

Easing the spring. And rapidly backwards and forwards

....

The early bees are assaulting and fumbling the flowers:

....

   They call it easing the Spring.

84

....

They call it easing the Spring: it is perfectly easy

....

If you have any strength in your thumb: like the bolt,

....

And the breech, and the cocking-piece, and the point of balance,

....

Which in our case we have not got; and the almond-blossom

....

Silent in all of the gardens and the bees going backwards and forwards,

....

   For today we have naming of parts.

Modeling
the voice or voices of the narrator
of a poem requires a close reading of
the original.

Five
Modeling Situation

Have you ever been engaged in doing something that required your outward attention while inwardly you were thinking about something else entirely? Write a poem that imitates this by using both an outward and an inner voice. Create a scenario in which a speaker (it does not have to be you) is in such a situation.

Fill out the chart showing the situation demanding outward attention and what is drawing the speaker's attention away from the outward situation. Include as much detail as you can in both columns.

What is the situation or the outward event that is happening?	What is the speaker thinking about during this event?

85

●◆Now write your poem using both inner and outer voices. Try making some words fit into both parts of the scenario, the way Reed did with the word *spring*. Since this is a spinoff poem and not an emulation, use any form you like for your poem.

In modeling, you choose an important element of the original scenario—in this case the prosaic and reflective voices—and write your own poem.

Crafting Memory

Writers mine memory. They draw openly on the events of their lives as a source for their work. Writers recall, reinvent, and refashion their lives into characters, places, and situations that have dramatic effect.

The raw stuff of memory, however, does not easily become poems and novels. Journals may contain fascinating seeds for stories and poems, but journals are not stories and poems without the vital element of craft. Craft gives shape to our formless memories and dreams. Craft allows writers to prune, to elaborate, to cut, to insert, using all the strategies that we call revision. These are the tools of the writer's craft.

In "Fern Hill," Dylan Thomas recreates the essence of his Welsh childhood on his aunt Anne's farm, where he spent his school holidays as a boy. Concentrate on the sounds and sights of the poem as you first read it. If possible, read it aloud or listen to someone reading it.

Response notes

Fern Hill
Dylan Thomas

Now as I was young and easy under the apple boughs
About the lilting house and happy as the grass was green,
   The night above the dingle starry,
     Time let me hail and climb
   Golden in the heydays of his eyes,
And honoured among wagons I was prince of the apple towns
And once below a time I lordly had the trees and leaves
     Trail with daisies and barley
   Down the rivers of the windfall light.

And as I was green and carefree, famous among the barns
About the happy yard and singing as the farm was home,
   In the sun that is young once only,
     Time let me play and be
   Golden in the mercy of his means,
And green and golden I was huntsman and herdsman, the calves
Sang to my horn, the foxes on the hills barked clear and cold,
     And the sabbath rang slowly
   In the pebbles of the holy streams.

All the sun long it was running, it was lovely, the hay
Fields high as the house, the tunes from the chimneys, it was air
   And playing, lovely and watery
     And fire green as grass.
   And nightly under the simple stars
As I rode to sleep the owls were bearing the farm away,
All the moon long I heard, blessed among stables, the nightjars
   Flying with the ricks, and the horses
     Flashing into the dark.

And then to awake, and the farm, like a wanderer white
With the dew, come back, the cock on his shoulder: it was all
   Shining, it was Adam and maiden,
     The sky gathered again
   And the sun grew round that very day.
So it must have been after the birth of the simple light
In the first, spinning place, the spellbound horses walking warm
   Out of the whinnying green stable
     On to the fields of praise.

88

Response notes

And honoured among foxes and pheasants by the gay house
Under the new made clouds and happy as the heart was long,
   In the sun born over and over,
      I ran my heedless ways,
   My wishes raced through the house high hay
And nothing I cared, at my sky blue trades, that time allows
In all his tuneful turning so few and such morning songs
   Before the children green and golden
      Follow him out of grace.

Nothing I cared, in the lamb white days, that time would take me
Up to the swallow thronged loft by the shadow of my hand,
   In the moon that is always rising,
     Nor that riding to sleep
   I should hear him fly with the high fields
And wake to the farm forever fled from the childless land.
Oh as I was young and easy in the mercy of his means,
     Time held me green and dying
   Though I sang in my chains like the sea.

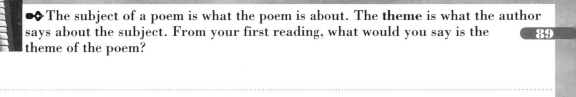 The subject of a poem is what the poem is about. The **theme** is what the author says about the subject. From your first reading, what would you say is the theme of the poem?

89

 "Fern Hill" takes close reading to appreciate all its subtleties, but the essence of it is available on first reading or hearing. What was the most vivid image for you during your first reading?

Certain kinds of images form the heart of Thomas' childhood memories. Find examples of images that fit the following categories: color, vegetation, animals, the sun, and the moon. Jot them down in the following chart. In the last column, add images that do not fit into these categories.

Color	Vegetation	Animals	Sun and Moon	Other

Which kinds of images are most powerful for you in evoking the scenes of Thomas' childhood? Explain why.

Noticing the kind of images a writer uses enables you to imagine the scenes for yourself as you read.

Two Childhood Memory

One of the characteristics of a well-crafted poem is the lack of any obvious signs of the craft itself. If you are immediately aware, on reading a poem, of the **rhyme scheme** or the **meter**, then you are likely to be less attentive to the meaning.

Look again at "Fern Hill" and observe the visual structure of the poem. Notice that each **stanza** makes a pattern on the page. Thomas has chosen a fluid, lilting pattern that echoes the childhood ecstasies he depicts in his poem. The important factor in crafting a poem is to choose the pattern that is right for the particular poem that you are writing.

●● The flowing, visually fluid pattern underscores the storyteller's quality of "Fern Hill." What other storytelling devices do you notice?

....

....

....

Imagine that you are writing the story of one of your childhood memories. Choose a place from your childhood that is dominated by one or two images. Cluster your memories, including as many concrete, sensory images as you can remember. What you do not remember, make up.

91

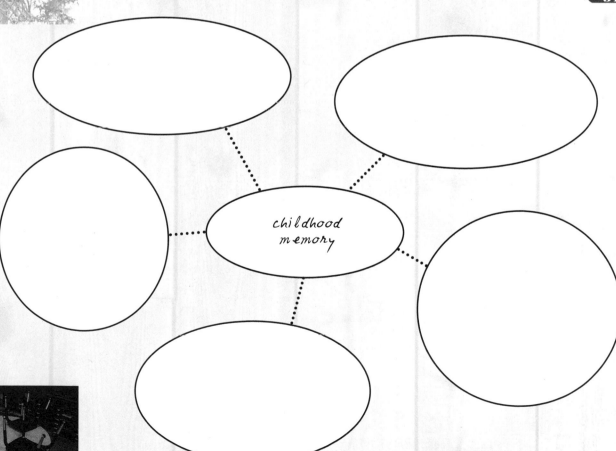

childhood memory

●◆ Write a poem about your childhood place. You have complete freedom here to construct your own pattern, simple or complex. If you like rhyme, use it. If **free verse** suits you, that will work, too. The main idea is that you, the poet, are the one to decide on what kind of crafting will make your memories of this place vivid for your readers.

Crafting memories into a poem requires careful attention to both images and form.

Three

The Language of Memory

In *A Portrait of the Artist as a Young Man*, James Joyce showed an interest in memory and language by recording a child's thoughts as he remembered and imagined them to be. In the following excerpt, Joyce introduces the main character, Stephen Dedalus. In your reading of this excerpt, do not worry about understanding all of the words. Many words are the child's made-up words; others are Irish colloquialisms or references to Irish history. Read to get a sense of what an author imagines a child's thoughts to be.

from ***A Portrait of the Artist as a Young Man*** by James Joyce

←—— *Response notes* ——→

Once upon a time and a very good time it was there was a moocow coming down along the road and this moocow that was down along the road met a nicens little boy named baby tuckoo. . . .

His father told him that story: his father looked at him through a glass: he had a hairy face.

He was baby tuckoo. The moocow came down the road where Betty Byrne lived: she sold lemon platt.

> *O, the wild rose blossoms*
> *On the little green place.*

He sang that song. That was his song.

O, the green wothe botheth.

When you wet the bed, first it is warm then it gets cold. His mother put on the oilsheet. That had the queer smell.

His mother had a nicer smell than his father. She played on the piano the sailor's hornpipe for him to dance. He danced:

> *Tralala lala,*
> *Tralala tralaladdy,*
> *Tralala lala,*
> *Tralala lala.*

Uncle Charles and Dante clapped. They were older than his father and mother but Uncle Charles was older than Dante.

Dante had two brushes in her press. The brush with the maroon velvet back was for Michael Davitt and the brush with the green velvet back was for Parnell. Dante gave him a cachou every time he brought her a piece of tissue paper.

The Vances lived in number seven. They had a different father and mother. They were Eileen's father and mother. When they were grown up he was going to marry Eileen. He hid under the table. His mother said:

—O, Stephen will apologise.

Dante said:

—O, if not, the eagles will come and pull out his eyes—

93

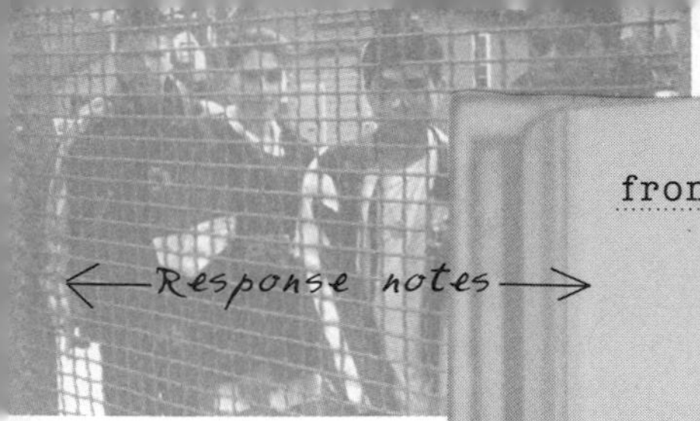

Pull out his eyes,
Apologise,
Apologise,
Pull out his eyes.

Apologise,
Pull out his eyes,
Pull out his eyes,
Apologise.

Joyce builds this scene in the way that young children actually perceive the world through their senses. Find examples of words or phrases denoting all of the senses:

Sight

Sound

Taste

Touch

Smell

➡️ Try your hand at recreating some of your own childhood. Begin by remembering an image from your childhood. Think of an idea that is important to you: family, sports, science, computers. Then imagine that you are three or four years old and write a scene in which you refer, even obliquely, to this idea. Include as many sensory details as you can.

95

Understanding the language of memory requires readers to be open to the author's style.

In another excerpt from *Portrait of the Artist as a Young Man*, Joyce attempts to recreate the thoughts of a slightly older Stephen. In this scene, set at the boarding school, Stephen is approached by Wells, one of the older boys.

---

from *A Portrait of the Artist as a Young Man* by James Joyce

—Tell us, Dedalus, do you kiss your mother before you go to bed?
Stephen answered:
—I do.
Wells turned to the other fellows and said:
—O, I say, here's a fellow says he kisses his mother every night before he goes to bed.
The other fellows stopped their game and turned round, laughing. Stephen blushed under their eyes and said:
—I do not.
Wells said:
—O, I say, here's a fellow says he doesn't kiss his mother before he goes to bed.
They all laughed again. Stephen tried to laugh with them. He felt his whole body hot and confused in a moment. What was the right answer to the question? He had given two and still Wells laughed. But Wells must know the right answer for he was in third of grammar. He tried to think of Wells's mother but he did not dare to raise his eyes to Wells's face. He did not like Wells's face. It was Wells who had shouldered him into the square ditch the day before because he would not swop his little snuffbox for Wells's seasoned hacking chestnut, the conqueror of forty. It was a mean thing to do; all the fellows said it was. And how cold and slimy the water had been! And a fellow had once seen a big rat jump plop into the scum.

The cold slime of the ditch covered his whole body; and, when the bell rang for study and the lines filed out of the playrooms, he felt the cold air of the corridor and staircase inside his clothes. He still tried to think what was the right answer. Was it right to kiss his mother or wrong to kiss his mother? What did that mean, to kiss? You put your face up like that to say goodnight and then his mother put her face down. That was to kiss. His mother put her lips on his cheek, her lips were soft and they wetted his cheek; and they made a tiny little noise: kiss. Why did people do that with their two faces?

✒ List the topics that Stephen explores as he withdraws from the taunting banter of the boys.

From what you have read about Stephen in these first two excerpts, what do you know about him as a person? What is he like? How does he appear to his family? To the other boys? Write a series of short descriptions of Stephen as the following people might see him.

His mother:

His father:

One of the boys at school:

A school master:

Stephen himself:

Through stream-of-consciousness writing, authors can reveal personality, recurrent thoughts, and character.

Daydreaming and Epiphanies

The passage from the previous lesson continues with Stephen sitting in a study hall. Rather than studying, however, he is reflecting on the big questions of life.

from *A Portrait of the Artist as a Young Man* by James Joyce

←—Response notes—→

Sitting in the study hall he opened the lid of his desk and changed the number pasted up inside from seventyseven to seventysix. But the Christmas vacation was very far away: but one time it would come because the earth moved round always.

There was a picture of the earth on the first page of his geography: a big ball in the middle of clouds. Fleming had a box of crayons and one night during free study he had coloured the earth green and the clouds maroon. That was like the two brushes in Dante's press, the brush with the green velvet back for Parnell and the brush with the maroon velvet back for Michael Davitt. But he had not told Fleming to colour them those colours. Fleming had done it himself.

He opened the geography to study the lesson; but he could not learn the names of places in America. Still they were all different places that had different names. They were all in different countries and the countries were in continents and the continents were in the world and the world was in the universe.

He turned to the flyleaf of the geography and read what he had written there: himself, his name and where he was.

> Stephen Dedalus
> Class of Elements
> Clongowes Wood College
> Sallins
> County Kildare
> Ireland
> Europe
> The World
> The Universe

That was in his writing: and Fleming one night for a cod had written on the opposite page:

> Stephen Dedalus is my name,
> Ireland is my nation.
> Clongowes is my dwelling place
> And heaven my expectation.

He read the verses backwards but then they were not poetry. Then he read the flyleaf from the bottom to the top till he came to his own name. That was he: and he read down the page again. What was after the universe? Nothing. But was there anything round the universe to show where it stopped before the nothing place began? It could not be

98

from **A Portrait of the Artist as a Young Man** by James Joyce

a wall but there could be a thin thin line there all round everything. It $\longleftarrow$ *Response notes* $\longrightarrow$
was very big to think about everything and everywhere. Only God
could do that. He tried to think what a big thought that must be but
he could think only of God. God was God's name just as his name was
Stephen. *Dieu* was the French for God and that was God's name too;
and when anyone prayed to God and said Dieu then God knew at once
that it was a French person that was praying. But though there were
different names for God in all the different languages in the world and
God understood what all the people who prayed said in their different
languages still God remained always the same God and God's real
name was God.

It made him very tired to think that way. It made him feel his
head very big.

The incident that Stephen experienced in this scene is called an *epiphany*. It is a
moment of insight when everything seems to come together, at least for that instant.
An epiphany may be as everyday as suddenly understanding a concept in science or
math or as overwhelming as envisioning your place in the universe.

Think of different moments in your life when you had a sense of understanding
something. Some suggestions:

- when you first knew someone was your friend
- when you first knew someone wasn't your friend
- when you understood your relationship to something bigger than you are—the
  galaxy, for instance
- when you were puzzling over a difficult concept in science or math, then,
  suddenly, "really got it"
- when you knew you weren't a little kid anymore

Think of others. Cluster or brainstorm your ideas here:

99

Now choose one of these moments. Jot down as many details as you can, such as

- how old you were
- what you were doing
- where you were
- what you were wearing
- what other people were there
  (or were you alone?)

●◆ Write an account of your epiphany. Jump right into the scene. Make the moment as clear as you can. Then stop. Do not explain or editorialize about why this moment was special. Just record it and stop.

An epiphany often marks an important turning point or realization in a novel. Such a moment usually occurs when a completely ordinary event takes on special significance.

Focus on the Writer: William Butler Yeats

William Butler Yeats (1865–1939) was one of the most significant writers of the century. He was the leader of the Irish Literary Revival, an ardent Irish nationalist, and a poet whose influence can be traced through the present century. T. S. Eliot wrote that Yeats "was one of those few whose history is the history of their own time, who are a part of the consciousness of an age which cannot be understood without them." Yeats was awarded the Nobel Prize for Literature in 1923.

Yeats' poems are quite complex; his themes were broad and he used a great deal of mystic symbolism. Yeats was a craftsman. He labored over every line, every reference, every image. In many ways he was part of the great transcendental movement of the nineteenth century, which looked to the world of the spirit as a way of informing the world of everyday realities.

The difficulties of reading Yeats are the difficulties inherent in reading any highly compressed, interrelated poems. Yeats thought of his entire body of work as part of a great architectural structure, a monument depicting his view of the world.

One Image and Symbol

Coole Park was an estate in Ireland owned by Lady Gregory, a woman who for twenty years provided Yeats with an idyllic summer place to live and work. In 1919, Yeats published "The Wild Swans at Coole" to commemorate what Coole Park meant to him. Read this poem first for the picture that Yeats paints with words.

Response notes

The Wild Swans at Coole
William Butler Yeats

The trees are in their autumn beauty,
The woodland paths are dry,
Under the October twilight the water
Mirrors a still sky;
Upon the brimming water among the stones
Are nine-and-fifty swans.

The nineteenth autumn has come upon me
Since I first made my count;
I saw, before I had well finished,
All suddenly mount
And scatter wheeling in great broken rings
Upon their clamorous wings.

I have looked upon those brilliant creatures,
And now my heart is sore.
All's changed since I, hearing at twilight,
The first time on this shore,
The bell-beat of their wings above my head,
Trod with a lighter tread.

Unwearied still, lover by lover,
They paddle in the cold
Companionable streams or climb the air;
Their hearts have not grown old;
Passion or conquest, wander where they will,
Attend upon them still.

But now they drift on the still water,
Mysterious, beautiful;
Among what rushes will they build,
By what lake's edge or pool
Delight men's eyes when I awake some day
To find they have flown away?

102

Reread the poem, marking the images that are most vivid for you. What **mood** or **tone** do these images convey? Do they carry a meaning for you beyond their obvious imagery?

●◆ Reread the last **stanza**. Explain what you think these lines mean in light of the entire poem.

●◆ What do you think the swans meant to Yeats?

An image becomes a symbol when it means both what it actually is and stands for something else as well. Writers often use recurrent symbols throughout their work.

Two The Dramatic Lyric

In "Coole Park, 1929," Yeats returns to the scene of the previous poem, ten years later. Yeats often wrote his poems as if they were being spoken to someone else, including other people in his poems, either as listeners or characters. This poem honors Lady Gregory, the owner of Coole Park. Each summer, Lady Gregory invited artists and writers to her home in Coole Park to work.

Response notes

Coole Park, 1929
William Butler Yeats

I meditate upon a swallow's flight,
Upon an aged woman and her house,
A sycamore and lime-tree lost in night
Although that western cloud is luminous,
Great works constructed there in nature's spite
For scholars and for poets after us,
Thoughts long knitted into a single thought,
A dance-like glory that those walls begot.

There Hyde before he had beaten into prose
That noble blade the Muses buckled on,
There one that ruffled in a manly pose
For all his timid heart, there that slow man,
That meditative man, John Synge, and those
Impetuous men, Shawe-Taylor and Hugh Lane,
Found pride established in humility,
A scene well set and excellent company.

They came like swallows and like swallows went,
And yet a woman's powerful character
Could keep a swallow to its first intent;
And half a dozen in formation there,
That seemed to whirl upon a compass-point,
Found certainty upon the dreaming air,
The intellectual sweetness of those lines
That cut through time or cross it withershins.

Here, traveller, scholar, poet, take your stand
When all those rooms and passages are gone,
When nettles wave upon a shapeless mound
And saplings root among the broken stone,
And dedicate—eyes bent upon the ground,
Back turned upon the brightness of the sun
And all the sensuality of the shade—
A moment's memory to that laurelled head.

●◆ What is the strongest image or idea for you in this poem after your first reading? Circle it and explain what it means to you below.

....

....

....

....

Now read the poem aloud. Read it as if you were just talking instead of reading. Like much of Yeats' poetry, this poem is written in **iambic pentameter**, a meter close to the rhythm of speech.

●◆ Write three sentences of your own that have the same meter, five **stresses** per line. Keep the same subject for all your lines. Make it sound as much like speech as you can within the confines of the line.

....

....

....

....

105

....

....

●◆ In the last lesson, you explored the symbolism of the swan. In this poem, Yeats writes about swallows. Write your ideas about how the meaning of the swallow image changes from stanza one to stanza three. Remember that a **symbol** is first the thing itself that then comes to stand for something else.

....

....

....

....

....

....

....

....

In a dramatic lyric, the poet explores ideas and images through the natural rhythms of the language of speech.

Read "The Second Coming" through once, listening to the **rhythm** and sound. Then read it again, making notations of your questions as well as possible meanings of phrases and lines. The title refers to the return of Christ as foretold in the Bible. *Spiritus Mundi* is Latin for the *spirit of the world*.

Response notes

The Second Coming
William Butler Yeats

Turning and turning in the widening gyre
The falcon cannot hear the falconer;
Things fall apart; the centre cannot hold;
Mere anarchy is loosed upon the world,
The blood-dimmed tide is loosed, and everywhere
The ceremony of innocence is drowned;
The best lack all conviction, while the worst
Are full of passionate intensity.

Surely some revelation is at hand;
Surely the Second Coming is at hand.
The Second Coming! Hardly are those words out
When a vast image out of *Spiritus Mundi*
Troubles my sight: somewhere in sands of the desert
A shape with lion body and the head of a man,
A gaze blank and pitiless as the sun,
Is moving its slow thighs, while all about it
Reel shadows of the indignant desert birds.
The darkness drops again; but now I know
That twenty centuries of stony sleep
Were vexed to nightmare by a rocking cradle,
And what rough beast, its hour come round at last,
Slouches towards Bethlehem to be born?

106

Use the space on the next page to make a drawing of as many of the images from the poem as you can. Integrate these images into a scene that depicts the mood and tone of the poem. Use colored markers, if possible.

Title:

●✦Explain what you drew and tell how your drawing is an interpretation of the poem.

Because of their aptness and their compression, some lines of poetry enter into the common language. You can hear lines from "The Second Coming" used regularly by politicians, journalists, even in advertising.

➥ What do these lines mean to you: "The best lack all conviction, while the worst / Are full of passionate intensity"?

➥ How might these lines be applied to what is happening in the world today: "Things fall apart; the centre cannot hold; / Mere anarchy is loosed upon the world"?

➥ Now write your ideas about the relevance of this poem today. Be as specific as you can in exploring ideas about how lines from this poem can be used to describe our times.

Recognizing and understanding great lines of poetry that have become part of our heritage is one of the benefits of reading widely.

Four

Poem as Autobiography

In "What Then?" we see Yeats in a familiar posture, obsessed by the process of growing old. He reflects on a question that nearly everyone asks at some point in his or her life.

What Then?
William Butler Yeats

His chosen comrades thought at school
He must grow a famous man;
He thought the same and lived by rule,
All his twenties crammed with toil;
"What then?" sang Plato's ghost. "What then?"

Everything he wrote was read,
After certain years he won
Sufficient money for his need,
Friends that have been friends indeed;
"What then?" sang Plato's ghost. "What then?"

All his happier dreams came true—
A small old house, wife, daughter, son,
Grounds where plum and cabbage grew,
Poets and Wits about him drew;
"What then?" sang Plato's ghost. "What then?"

"The work is done," grown old he thought,
"According to my boyish plan;
Let the fools rage, I swerved in naught,
Something to perfection brought";
But louder sang that ghost, "What then?"

●◆ How would you describe the feeling that Yeats conveys in the simple refrain "What then?"?

●✧ Plato believed that the ultimate meaning of life was discoverable through the process of questioning, a form that has come to be known as "platonic dialogues." In this poem, the question that forms the refrain of the first three stanzas is changed in the last stanza. How is it different from the earlier refrain? Comment on the meaning of the last line of the poem.

....

....

....

....

●✧ Think about your own life, now at the threshold of leaving high school and entering a new phase. What would your friends say now about who you might become? Write your own poem, using Yeats' opening as a way of getting started. Supply your own refrain. Write three stanzas.

....

....

....

....

....

....

....

....

....

....

....

....

In autobiographical poems, the poet reveals glimpses of ideas about the meaning of life.

Five
The Artistic Process

The following essay appeared as part of Yeats' introduction to *The Oxford Book of Modern Verse*. In it, Yeats expounds on his beliefs about what goes into the artistic process. Make note of your questions as well as your own ideas about art as you read.

from the Introduction to *The Oxford Book of Modern Verse*
by William Butler Yeats

The progress of an artist is a continual self-sacrifice, a continual extinction of personality.

There remains to define this process of depersonalization and its relation to the sense of tradition. It is in this depersonalization that art may be said to approach the condition of science. I shall, therefore, invite you to consider, as a suggestive analogy, the action which takes place when a bit of finely filiated platinum is introduced into a chamber containing oxygen and sulphur dioxide. . . .

When the two gases . . . are mixed in the presence of a filament of platinum, they form sulphurous acid. This combination takes place only if the platinum is present; nevertheless the newly formed acid contains no trace of platinum, and the platinum itself is apparently unaffected; has remained inert, neutral, and unchanged. The mind of the poet is the shred of platinum. It may partly or exclusively operate upon the experience of the man himself; but, the more perfect the artist, the more completely separate in him will be the man who suffers and the mind which creates; the more perfectly will the mind digest and transmute the passions which are its material.

The experience, you will notice, the elements which enter the presence of the transforming catalyst, are of two kinds: emotions and feelings. The effect of a work of art upon the person who enjoys it is an experience different in kind from any experience not of art. It may be formed out of one emotion, or may be a combination of several; and various feelings, inhering for the writer in particular words or phrases or images, may be added to compose the final result. Or great poetry may be made without the direct use of any emotion whatever: composed out of feelings solely. . . .

The poet's mind is in fact a receptacle for seizing and storing up numberless feelings, phrases, images, which remain there until all the particles which can unite to form a new compound are present together.

If you compare several representative passages of the greatest poetry you see how great is the variety of types of combination, and also how completely any semi-ethical criterion of "sublimity" misses the mark. For it is not the "greatness," the intensity, of the emotions, the components, but the intensity of the artistic process, the pressure, so to speak, under which the fusion takes place, that counts.

←—Response notes—→

111

Select three lines which you find provocative and write them in column one. In column two, explain your ideas about what these lines mean.

Lines from the essay	What these lines mean

●◆ Here is the first line of Yeats' essay again: "The progress of an artist is a continual self-sacrifice, a continual extinction of personality." In light of this essay and the poems you have read by Yeats, explain your ideas about this statement. Feel free to take issue with his views, but be sure to explain your reasons for doing so.

A writer's views about art provide insight into the art itself.

113

Essentials of Reading

It is great to have strong opinions about what you read, but are you certain that you truly understand what you are reading? Have you given the author a chance to show you something new or interest you in something old? Have you listened to the author's message and considered the author's themes? If not, you have not really worked your way through every essential of reading.

In this unit, you will learn some techniques that will help you better relate to and understand what you read. These techniques include making predictions, drawing inferences, and finding themes. In the lessons that follow you will be asked to explore these and other reading essentials.

One
Thinking With the Writer

When you first see a story, essay, or poem, what do you think? Your expectations can help you make predictions about the text. Predictions help you read actively. As you read, you wonder about what will happen next and read to find out. That leads to more predictions and answers.

●◆ Before you read "Trail of the Green Blazer," think about the title. What kind of story do you think it will be: a mystery, a thriller, a romance? What do you think the "Green Blazer" is?

Read Narayan's story to find out, and as you read, make predictions about the outcome.

"Trail of the Green Blazer" by R. K. Narayan

←— *Response notes* —→

The Green Blazer stood out prominently under the bright sun and blue sky. In all that jostling crowd one could not help noticing it. Villagers in shirts and turbans, townsmen in coats and caps, beggars bare-bodied and women in multicoloured saris were thronging the narrow passage between the stalls and moving in great confused masses, but still the Green Blazer could not be missed. The jabber and babble of the marketplace was there, as people harangued, disputed prices, haggled or greeted each other; over it all boomed the voice of a Bible-preacher, and when he paused for breath, from another corner the loudspeaker of a health van amplified on malaria and tuberculosis. Over and above it all the Green Blazer seemed to cry out an invitation. Raju could not ignore it. It was not in his nature to ignore such a persistent invitation. He kept himself half-aloof from the crowd; he could not afford to remain completely aloof or keep himself in it too conspicuously. Wherever he might be, he was harrowed by the fear of being spotted by a policeman; today he wore a loincloth and was bare-bodied, and had wound an enormous turban over his head, which overshadowed his face completely, and he hoped that he would be taken for a peasant from a village.

He sat on a stack of cast-off banana stalks beside a shop awning and watched the crowd. When he watched a crowd he did it with concentration. It was his professional occupation. Constitutionally he was an idler and had just the amount of energy to watch in a crowd and put his hand into another person's pocket. It was a gamble, of course. Sometimes he got nothing out of a venture, counting himself lucky if he came out with his fingers intact. Sometimes he picked up a fountain pen, and the "receiver" behind the Municipal Office would not offer even four annas for it, and there was always the danger of being traced through it. Raju promised himself that someday he would leave fountain pens alone; he wouldn't touch one even if it were

"Trail of the Green Blazer" by R. K. Narayan

←— Response notes —→

presented to him on a plate; they were too much bother—inky, leaky, and next to worthless if one could believe what the receiver said about them. Watches were in the same category, too.

What Raju loved most was a nice, bulging purse. If he saw one he picked it up with the greatest deftness. He took the cash in it, flung it far away and went home with the satisfaction that he had done his day's job well. He splashed a little water over his face and hair and tidied himself up before walking down the street again as a normal citizen. He bought sweets, books and slates for his children, and occasionally a jacket-piece for his wife, too. He was not always easy in mind about his wife. When he went home with too much cash, he had always to take care to hide it in an envelope and shove it under a roof tile. Otherwise she asked too many questions and made herself miserable. She liked to believe that he was reformed and earned the cash he showed her as commission; she never bothered to ask what the commissions were for: a commission seemed to her something absolute.

STOP AND PREDICT

•◆What do you think Raju is going to do?

Raju jumped down from the banana stack and followed the Green Blazer, always keeping himself three steps behind. It was a nicely calculated distance, acquired by intuition and practise. The distance must not be so much as to obscure the movement of the other's hand to and from his purse, nor so close as to become a nuisance and create suspicion. It had to be finely balanced and calculated—the same sort of calculations as carry a *shikari* through his tracking of game and see him safely home again. Only this hunter's task was more complicated. The hunter in the forest could count his day a success if he laid his quarry flat; but here one had to extract the heart out of the quarry without injuring it.

Raju waited patiently, pretending to be examining some rolls of rush mat, while the Green Blazer spent a considerable length of time drinking a coconut at a nearby booth. It looked as though he would not move again at all. After sucking all the milk in the coconut, he seemed to wait interminably for the nut to be split and the soft white kernel scooped out with a knife. The sight of the white kernel scooped and disappearing into the other's mouth made Raju, too, crave for it. But he suppressed the thought: it would be inept to be spending one's time drinking and eating while one was professionally occupied; the other might slip away and be lost forever . . . . Raju saw the other take out his black purse and start a debate with the coconut-seller over the price of coconuts. He had a thick, sawing voice which disconcerted Raju. It sounded like the growl of a tiger, but what jungle-

←— *Response notes* —→

hardened hunter ever took a step back because a tiger's growl sent his heart racing involuntarily! The way the other haggled didn't appeal to Raju either; it showed a mean and petty temperament . . . too much fondness for money. Those were the narrow-minded troublemakers who made endless fuss when a purse was lost . . . . The Green Blazer moved after all. He stopped before a stall flying coloured balloons. He bought a balloon after an endless argument with the shopman—a further demonstration of his meanness. He said, "This is for a motherless boy. I have promised it to him. If it bursts or gets lost before I go home, he will cry all night, and I wouldn't like it at all."

Raju got his chance when the other passed through a narrow stile, where people were passing four-thick in order to see a wax model of Mahatma Gandhi reading a newspaper.

Fifteen minutes later Raju was examining the contents of the purse. He went away to a secluded spot, behind a disused well. Its crumbling parapet seemed to offer an ideal screen for his activities. The purse contained ten rupees in coins and twenty in currency notes and a few annas in nickel. Raju tucked the annas at his waist in his loincloth. "Must give them to some beggars," he reflected generously. There was a blind fellow yelling his life out at the entrance to the fair and nobody seemed to care. People seemed to have lost all sense of sympathy these days. The thirty rupees he bundled into a knot at the end of his turban and wrapped this again round his head. It would see him through the rest of the month. He could lead a clean life for at least a fortnight and take his wife and children to a picture.

Now the purse lay limp within the hollow of his hand. It was only left for him to fling it into the well and dust off his hand and then he might walk among princes with equal pride at heart. He peeped into the well. It had a little shallow water at the bottom. The purse might float, and a floating purse could cause the worst troubles on earth. He opened the flap of the purse in order to fill it up with pebbles before drowning it. Now, through the slit at its side, he saw a balloon folded and tucked away. "Oh, this he bought. . . ." He remembered the other's talk about the motherless child. "What a fool to keep this in the purse," Raju reflected. "It is the carelessness of parents that makes young ones suffer," he ruminated angrily. For a moment he paused over a picture of the growling father returning home and the motherless one waiting at the door for the promised balloon, and this growling man feeling for his purse . . . and, oh! It was too painful!

STOP AND PREDICT

●❖What will Raju do with the purse and the balloon?

....

....

....

"Trail of the Green Blazer" by R. K. Narayan

Raju almost sobbed at the thought of the disappointed child—the motherless boy. There was no one to comfort him. Perhaps this ruffian would beat him if he cried too long. The Green Blazer did not look like one who knew the language of children. Raju was filled with pity at the thought of the young child—perhaps of the same age as his second son. Suppose his wife were dead . . . (personally it might make things easier for him, he need not conceal his cash under the roof); he overcame this thought as an unworthy side issue. If his wife should die it would make him very sad indeed and tax all his ingenuity to keep his young ones quiet . . . . That motherless boy must have his balloon at any cost, Raju decided. The thing to do would be to put it back into the empty purse and slip it into the other's pocket.

The Green Blazer was watching the heckling that was going on as the Bible-preacher warmed up to his subject. A semicircle was asking, "Where is your God?" There was a hubbub. Raju sidled up to the Green Blazer. The purse with the balloon (only) tucked into it was in his palm. He'd slip it back into the other's pocket.

Raju realized his mistake in a moment. The Green Blazer caught hold of his arm and cried, "Pickpocket!" The hecklers lost interest in the Bible and turned their attention to Raju, who tried to look appropriately outraged. He cried, "Let me go." The other, without giving a clue to what he proposed, shot out his arm and hit him on the cheek. It almost blinded him. For a fraction of a second Raju lost his awareness of where and even who he was. When the dark mist lifted and he was able to regain his vision, the first figure he noticed in the foreground was the Green Blazer, looming, as it seemed, over the whole landscape. His arms were raised ready to strike again. Raju cowered at the sight. He said, "I . . . I was trying to put back your purse." The other gritted his teeth in fiendish merriment and crushed the bones of his arm. The crowd roared with laughter and badgered him. Somebody hit him again on the head.

Even before the Magistrate Raju kept saying, "I was only trying to put back the purse." And everyone laughed. It became a stock joke in the police world. Raju's wife came to see him in jail and said, "You have brought shame to us," and wept.

Raju replied indignantly, "Why? I was only trying to put it back."

He served his term of eighteen months and came back into the world—not quite decided what he should do with himself. He told himself, "If ever I pick up something again, I shall make sure I don't have to put it back." For now he believed God had gifted the likes of him with only one-way deftness. Those fingers were not meant to put anything back.

117

●❖ How did your predictions help you become involved in the world of Narayan's story? Explain.

....

....

....

The expectations that we bring to a story help us make predictions before and during reading.

The expectations that we bring to a text can also help us make **inferences**. Inferences are reasonable conclusions that we can make using the details in the story. Readers make inferences about characters' personalities and motivation, setting, and plot. When you read "Trail of the Green Blazer," you might have used the author's name and the details in the first paragraph such as "saris," "turban," or the crowded marketplace to infer that the story is set in India.

Authors do not make inferences for readers; instead they assume that we will actively construct a level of meaning beyond the mere words on the page. For example, we know that Raju picks Green Blazer's pocket, empties the purse, and then discovers the balloon. We also know that he decides to return the balloon. What Narayan does not tell us, though, is why Raju cares that a child might have to go without his balloon. That is left for us to infer.

Review the notes you made while reading "Trail of the Green Blazer." Then make some inferences about the two central characters. On the chart, list words or phrases for Raju and Green Blazer in the left column. In the right column, make an inference about what the adjective shows about the character.

action or quotation	inference
Green Blazer buys a balloon	he has a soft spot for a child

Making inferences about a story's characters will help you understand the characters' actions and motivations.

Three Thinking Theme

When you think about the **theme** of a story, you go beyond the boundaries of the story itself. The theme is the author's generalization about life or human nature. A single story may have several themes.

To discuss the themes of a story, you must consider both the subject and what the author has to say about the subject. For example, one subject in "Trail of the Green Blazer" could be sympathy for others. To state the theme, ask yourself, "What is Narayan's attitude about sympathy for others"?

●✦ Write a sentence that states the theme of "Trail of the Green Blazer," combining the subject of the story and Narayan's attitude toward it.

Read "Homage for Isaac Babel." As you read, annotate the selection by circling phrases and sentences that might relate to Lessing's themes.

"Homage for Isaac Babel" by Doris Lessing

The day I had promised to take Catherine down to visit my young friend Philip at his school in the country, we were to leave at eleven, but she arrived at nine. Her blue dress was new, and so were her fashionable shoes. Her hair had just been done. She looked more than ever like a pink-and-gold Renoir girl who expects everything from life.

← Response notes →

Catherine lives in a white house overlooking the sweeping brown tides of the river. She helped me clean up my flat with a devotion which said that she felt small flats were altogether more romantic than large houses. We drank tea, and talked mainly about Philip, who, being fifteen, has pure stern tastes in everything from food to music. Catherine looked at the books lying around his room, and asked if she might borrow the stories of Isaac Babel to read on the train. Catherine is thirteen. I suggested she might find them difficult, but she said: "Philip reads them, doesn't he?"

During the journey I read newspapers and watched her pretty frowning face as she turned the pages of Babel, for she was determined to let nothing get between her and her ambition to be worthy of Philip.

At the school, which is charming, civilized, and expensive, the two children walked together across green fields, and I followed, seeing how the sun gilded their bright friendly heads turned towards each other as they talked. In Catherine's left hand she carried the stories of Isaac Babel.

After lunch we went to the pictures. Philip allowed it to be seen that he thought going to the pictures just for the fun of it was not worthy of intelligent people, but he made the concession, for our sakes. For his sake we chose the more serious of the two films that were showing in the little town. It was about a good priest who helped criminals in New York. His goodness, however, was not enough to prevent one of them from being sent to the gas chamber; and Philip and I waited with Catherine in the dark until she had stopped crying and could face the light of a golden evening.

At the entrance of the cinema the doorman was lying in wait for anyone who had red eyes. Grasping Catherine by her suffering arm, he said bitterly: "Yes, why are you crying? He had to be punished for his crime, didn't he?" Catherine stared at him, incredulous. Philip rescued her by saying with disdain: "Some people don't know right from wrong even when it's *demonstrated* to them." The doorman turned his attention to the next red-eyed emerger from the dark; and we went on together to the station, the children silent because of the cruelty of the world.

Finally Catherine said, her eyes wet again: "I think it's all absolutely beastly, and I can't bear to think about it." And Philip said: "But we've got to think about it, don't you see, because if we don't it'll just go on and *on*, don't you see?"

In the train going back to London I sat beside Catherine. She had the stories open in front of her, but she said: "Philip's awfully lucky. I wish I went to that school. Did you notice that girl who said hullo to him in the garden? They must be great friends. I wish my mother would let me have a dress like that, it's *not* fair."

"I thought it was too old for her."

"Oh, *did* you?"

Soon she bent her head again over the book, but almost at once she lifted it to say: "Is he a very famous writer?"

"He's a marvelous writer, brilliant, one of the very best."

"Why?"

"Well, for one thing he's so simple. Look how few words he uses, and how strong his stories are."

"I see. Do you know him? Does he live in London?"

"Oh no, he's dead."

"Oh. Then why did you—I thought he was alive, the way you talked."

"I'm sorry, I suppose I wasn't thinking of him as dead."

"When did he die?"

"He was murdered. About twenty years ago, I suppose."

"Twenty years." Her hands began the movement of pushing the book over to me, but then relaxed. "I'll be fourteen in November," she stated, sounding threatened, while her eyes challenged me.

I found it hard to express my need to apologize, but before I could speak, she said patiently attentive again: "You said he was murdered?"

"Yes."

"I expect the person who murdered him felt sorry when he discovered he had murdered a famous writer."

"Yes, I expect so."

"Was he old when he was murdered?"

"No, quite young really."

"Well, that was bad luck, wasn't it?"

"Yes, I suppose it was bad luck."

"Which do you think is the very best story here? I mean, in your honest opinion, the very very best one?"

"Homage for Isaac Babel" by Doris Lessing

I chose the story about killing the goose. She read it slowly, while I ←—— *Response notes* ——→
sat waiting, wishing to take it from her, wishing to protect this
charming little person from Isaac Babel.

When she had finished, she said: "Well, some of it I don't
understand. He's got a funny way of looking at things. Why should a
man's legs in boots look like *girls*?" She finally pushed the book over
at me, and said: "I think it's all morbid."

"But you have to understand the kind of life he had. First, he was
a Jew in Russia. That was bad enough. Then his experience was all
revolution and civil war and. . . ."

But I could see these words bounding off the clear glass of her
fiercely denying gaze; and I said: "Look, Catherine, why don't you try
again when you're older? Perhaps you'll like him better then?"

She said gratefully: "Yes, perhaps that would be best. After all,
Philip is two years older than me, isn't he?"

A week later I got a letter from Catherine.

> Thank you very much for being kind enough to take
> me to visit Philip at his school. It was the most lovely
> day in my whole life. I am extremely grateful to you
> for taking me. I have been thinking about the Hoodlum
> Priest. That was a film which demonstrated to me
> beyond any shadow of doubt that Capital Punishment
> is a Wicked Thing, and I shall never forget what I
> learned that afternoon, and the lessons of it will be
> with me all my life. I have been meditating about what
> you said about Isaac Babel, the famed Russian short
> story writer, and I now see that the conscious
> simplicity of his style is what makes him, beyond the
> shadow of a doubt, the great writer that he is, and
> now in my school compositions I am endeavoring to
> emulate him so as to learn a conscious simplicity
> which is the only basis for a really brilliant writing
> style. Love, Catherine. P.S. Has Philip said anything
> about my party? I wrote but he hasn't answered.
> Please find out if he is coming or if he just forgot to
> answer my letter. I hope he comes, because sometimes
> I feel I shall die if he doesn't. P.P.S. Please don't tell
> him I said anything, because I should die if he knew.
> Love, Catherine.

●◆ **What do you think Lessing wants you to remember most from this story?**

●◆ **Now write a sentence that summarizes the theme.**

To find the theme of a piece, look at the subject of the story. Then try to analyze the author's attitude toward the subject.

Four Doubling Back

Sometimes you will read a book or article or story and like it so much that you feel compelled to return to the piece again for another reading. Other times you will read something and are so puzzled that you throw it down in frustration. Rereading and reflecting on the theme and ideas of a work are essential to understanding what you read.

Reread "Homage to Isaac Babel." Underline or circle anything in the story that you can relate to your own life.

➡ Reflect on the characters in the story. Which one do you find it easiest to relate to: Catherine, Philip, or the narrator? Why?

> Rereading and reflecting are essential to understand what an author means by a work and how the work relates to your own life.

Read your reflections to a partner and compare what aspect of the story you related to your own lives. Discuss how your own experiences influenced your view of the story.

Five
Author's Purpose

Why has the author written the piece? What is his or her intent? Understanding the author's purpose is a key part of reading. As you read this piece by Frank O'Connor, make some notes about his purpose. Which parts are enlightening? Which parts are interesting or persuasive?

from **"Writing a Story—One Man's Way"** by Frank O'Connor

←—— *Response notes* ——→

Once when I was lecturing in America and, as usual, could not think of a title for my lecture, someone advertised it as "One Man's Way," and that seemed to me such a good title that I wanted to use it again. Because short-story writing is my job, and, as all of us who write stories will know, there is only one way to do a job and that is the way you do it yourself.

I am dealing here with one man's way of writing a story, and the thing this man likes best in the story is the story itself. A story begins when someone grabs you by the lapel and says: "The most extraordinary thing happened to me yesterday." I don't like the sort of story that begins with someone saying: "I don't know if it's a matter of any interest to you but I'd like to describe my emotions while observing sunset last evening." I am not saying the second man may not have important things to say, things far more important than those the first has to say, but that particular tone gives me the shivers. I like the feeling that the story-teller has something to communicate, and if he doesn't communicate it he'll bust.

The story can be anything from the latest shaggy dog story to an incident so complex that for the rest of your life you will be wondering what the meaning of it was. Let me tell you a story that has made me wonder. Once when my father and I were staying in a little seaside place in County Cork we got into a conversation with a farmer whose son had emigrated to America. There he had married a North of Ireland girl, and soon after she fell very ill and was advised to go home and recuperate. Before she went to her own family she spent six weeks with her husband's family in County Cork, and they all fell in love with her. It was only when she had left that they discovered from friends in America that their son had been dead before she left America at all.

"Now, why would she do a thing like that to us?" the old farmer asked, and for years I asked myself the same question.

Sometimes a story leaves you with a question. Sometimes it answers a question that has been in your mind. I had always felt ashamed of the horrible, snobbish attitude I had adopted to my own father and mother when I was growing up—an attitude for which there was no justification. Then a couple of years ago my wife and I were walking in the little American city where we lived and we came on my son standing at a street corner with a girl—his first girl. I was wearing an Aran Island beret which I found very comfortable in the American winters. Instantly his face grew black and her face lit up,

123

and it was as plain as though the pair of them had said it that he was mortified by the spectacle of his degraded old father who knew no better than to wear a knitted cap in the street, and she was thrilled at the thought of a father who did not dress like every other American father.

At that moment I understood my own horrible snobbery, and realized that falling in love always means being a bit ashamed of one's own parents and a bit enthusiastic about others'. At the age of seventeen we all have ambitions to be adopted.

But before I wrote that story, or would allow any student of mine to write it, I had to see exactly what it looked like. I find it easier to see it if it is written in four lines. Four is only an ideal, of course; I don't really quarrel with five, and sometimes a difficult subject may require six. But four is the best length; four is a seed: anything more is a cutting from somebody else's garden.

Do you agree with O'Connor's assertion that anything more than four lines is "a cutting from somebody else's garden"? Explain.

124

Think about the Narayan and Lessing stories. Choose one of them and then rewrite it as a four-line narrative. When you have finished, compare your work with that of a fellow student.

Understanding the author's purpose will help you understand the author's message.

125

Experiencing the Story

How the story is told influences how we experience it. For example, if the events of a story are told in the present tense, it may be easier to become involved in the actions and thoughts of characters. We may find ourselves more remote or distant from the events of a story told in the past tense. While reading a story, we may find ourselves involved in a double experience—remaining detached (knowing we are reading) and yet becoming involved (experiencing what is taking place) at the same time. We may participate in the characters' adventures, worry about their futures, and feel satisfaction when they succeed. All this is an illusion, of course. The story has an ending that has been written long before we read it. However, the storyteller uses various techniques to unroll time and action before us, creating the illusion that the story is happening as we read it. The ways we experience the story—the way we bring life into it—is guided by the writer's particular techniques.

One Tension and Anticipation

Our knowledge or sense of what is about to happen allows us to anticipate, and anticipation is a form of experiencing the story. **Tension** in a story exists because something is unresolved. When the writer prolongs and postpones the resolution, we anticipate what will happen. The most obvious way to create anticipation is simply by describing the tensions that exist:

> Version One: Eric Denton knew the trip would be a long one. He imagined his mother would have deep worry lines thick in her brow, that she would finger the pocket of her apron before she turned back into the kitchen. All this Eric knew from the sound of his heart beating.

For you to experience anticipation and the events, the writer needs to dramatize the tension. Here is another version of the same scene:

> Version Two: Sweat trickles down his spine as the rain taps against his shoulder. "Momma's worryin' herself into a sickness," Eric's thinking as he breaks into a run. The leaves whirl overhead. "Hurry, hurry, hurry," drums in his head as he dodges in and out of traffic, avoiding cars and the looks of drivers bleating their horns at him.

What are the differences in your reading experience in version one (which tells) and version two (which dramatizes)?

As you read the following episode from Sebastian Faulks' novel about World War I, mark places where tension is created. The following episode takes place in the tunnels dug beneath the trenches.

126

from ***Birdsong*** by Sebastian Faulks

← *Response notes* →

The tunnel became narrower and they were obliged to go down on all fours again. The front men suddenly stopped, causing the others to crush together behind them in the darkness.

"I think they've heard something," Crawshaw whispered into Stephen's ear. "No one move."

The men lay huddled in the tube of earth as Evans fumbled in his pack and squeezed through them to get up to his three colleagues at the front. After a whispered consultation, Evans squirmed forward to a piece of dry wall and stuck a flat disc against it, into which he plugged a stethoscope. Crawshaw raised a finger to his lips and made a downward motion with both hands. The others lay flat on the floor of the tunnel. Stephen felt a stone against his cheek, and tried to shift his head. He was lodged up against the leg of someone he could not see and had to stay where he was. He could feel his heart moving slowly against his ribs.

Evans lay tight against the tunnel wall, like an unwashed and unqualified doctor listening for signs of hostile life.

Stephen closed his eyes. He wondered whether, if he stayed in this position long enough, he might drift off to a final sleep. The agitation of the other men prevented him from sliding into his own thoughts. He could sense their fear through the tension of the bodies that pressed against his. It was their passivity that made it difficult; even against the guns they had some chance of riposte, but beneath this weight they were helpless.

from *Birdsong* by Sebastian Faulks

←—Response notes—→

Evans eventually pulled the stethoscope out of his ears and folded it back into his pocket. He shook his head and pursed his lips. He whispered his report to his lieutenant, who in turn put his mouth to Stephen's ear.

"Can't hear anything. It may have been shellfire from the surface. We're going to press on."

The men on the floor of the tunnel stirred and dragged themselves back again into their crouching positions, in which they could again advance deeper.

Stephen could feel himself sweating. He could tell by the stench from the bodies packed in around him that he was not the only one. Trench conditions had improved, but not to the extent of providing the men with means of washing, even in hot weather.

The roof of the tunnel began to lift a little, and the smaller men, such as Evans and Jones, were able to walk upright. They came to a junction where the miners' lieutenant, Lorimer, issued instructions. The main digging party would proceed straight to the listening chamber; the others would go into one of the fighting tunnels alongside, the entrance to which he was now able to point out.

Stephen smiled to himself as he saw the expressions on the faces of his men. They exaggerated their reluctance into comic grimaces, but he knew from his own experience that it was real enough. He was glad he was going into what, presumably, would be the largest section of tunnel. He had no fear of going forward provided he felt he could get back. What had frightened him underground with Weir was when the earth fell behind them and he had for a moment thought he would not be able to turn round.

Crawshaw checked that his men had their grenades and rifles. He himself carried a revolver, which he waved dangerously toward the tunnel entrances. Stephen guessed he was trying to show them how fearless he was. Perhaps they believed him.

He watched them depart. He remembered the feelings of tenderness he used to have for the men when they went into battle or on patrol; he used to imagine their lives and hopes, their homes and their families, the little worlds they carried on their backs and in their minds. He could remember this compassion, but he no longer felt it.

His own party was about twenty-five yards short of the main listening chamber when Lorimer again came to a halt and raised his finger to his lips.

Stephen inhaled tightly. He was beginning to regret having come down. Either Lorimer was nervous, and was turning a routine inspection into something protracted and unpleasant, or else there was real danger. Evans had taken his listening set into the adjacent tunnel. Jack Firebrace was summoned by Lorimer to place his ear against the wall.

Jack covered the other ear with his hand and closed his eyes for better concentration. For half a minute they all stood motionless. In the light of a miner's lamp, Stephen stared with minute intensity at the grain of a piece of timber about six inches from his face. He

127

←—Response notes—→ traced the tiny lines and indentations. He imagined how it would curl beneath a plane.

Jack pulled back his head from the wall and wheeled to face Lorimer. His urgent whisper was audible to all of them.

"There's footsteps, going back toward their lines. They've got a tunnel west and about ten feet up."

As incidents accumulate, we experience the action along with the characters and have a heightened sense that something will happen.

Use the following chart to record how Faulks dramatizes tension and how you experience the story as a result. In the left column, identify the technique used. Dialogue, actions, and foreshadowing are techniques that are often used to build tension. In the center column, record words or phrases from the passage that demonstrate the technique. On the right, explain the experience this creates or the effect on you.

Technique Used	Quotation	Experience Created
descriptions of the close confines of the tunnel	"The men lay huddled in the tube of earth" "crushed together", and "tunnel became narrower"	dramatize how dangerous the situation is and anticipate that the tunnel will collapse
sentence structure	"Stephen inhaled tightly."	short sentences stop the action and build suspense

128

Share your chart with a partner. Compare the techniques found and discuss how effective Faulks was in dramatizing the situation.

●◆ Write a description of an incident from your own experience. Try to dramatize the tension that surrounded the incident. Use the techniques from Faulks' writing to help your reader experience the action.

129

A writer
dramatizes the tensions of
various actions and events so the reader
will anticipate the outcome and
experience the events along with
the characters.

Two Empathy and Sympathy

Stories encourage you to immerse yourself in characters' experiences. When you identify with one or more of the characters and understand their situation, you are experiencing empathy.

Reread the excerpt from *Birdsong*. Highlight places where you identify with the situation or actually experience a physical sensation that the character is feeling. For example, claustrophobia might result as you read descriptions of the narrowness and darkness of the tunnel.

●◆ What did you empathize with most in the excerpt? What techniques does Faulks employ to evoke your empathy?

130

●◆ Try your hand at creating the next scene in the tunnel. Continue from the last sentence of the selection. Emphasize the characters' feelings and sensations that will evoke the strongest reaction from the reader.

Readers respond empathetically to various aspects of the story. The writer encourages them to experience the characters' situation.

Three

Observer and Participant

Our experience with a story derives in part from whether the writer positions us as participants or observers in the unfolding events. In most stories, you will find that the writer moves you back and forth.

In the following short story by D. H. Lawrence, a **third-person** narrator tells the story of Egbert's life with his wife and small daughters. As you read, keep track in your response notes of the times you feel that you are standing at a distance observing the scene, and when you feel in the middle of the action, as a participant.

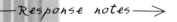

from **"England, My England"** by D. H. Lawrence

← *Response notes* →

He was working on the edge of the common, beyond the small brook that ran in the dip at the bottom of the garden, carrying the garden path in continuation from the plank bridge on to the common. He had cut the rough turf and bracken, leaving the grey, dryish soil bare. But he was worried because he could not get the path straight, there was a pleat between his brows. He had set up his sticks, and taken the sights between the big pine trees, but for some reason everything seemed wrong. He looked again, straining his keen blue eyes, that had a touch of the Viking in them, through the shadowy pine trees as through a doorway, at the green-grassed garden-path rising from the shadow of alders by the log bridge up to the sunlit flowers. Tall white and purple columbines, and the butt-end of the old Hampshire cottage that crouched near the earth amid flowers, blossoming in the bit of shaggy wildness round about.

There was a sound of children's voices calling and talking: high, childish, girlish voices, slightly didactic and tinged with domineering: "If you don't come quick, nurse, I shall run out there to where there are snakes." And nobody had the *sang-froid* to reply: "Run then, little fool." It was always "No, darling. Very well, darling. In a moment, darling. Darling, you *must* be patient."

His heart was hard with disillusion: a continual gnawing and resistance. But he worked on. What was there to do but submit!

The sunlight blazed down upon the earth, there was a vividness of flamy vegetation, of fierce seclusion amid the savage peace of the commons. Strange how the savage England lingers in patches: as here, amid these shaggy gorse commons, and marshy, snake-infested places near the foot of the south downs. The spirit of place lingering on primeval, as when the Saxons came, so long ago.

131

Now read a passage from an Iris Murdoch novel that also relies on a third-person narrator to tell the story. Again, mark where you are participant and where you are an observer.

←─── Response notes ───→

Some while later Marian began to walk back through the wrecked gardens. The moon had been quenched in cloud. She had not been outside. She had had to detach herself from the archway almost by pulling her hands off the stone, so alarming did everything seem both in front of her and behind her. She had never felt quite like this before, alone in her own mind; and yet not quite alone, for somewhere in the big darkness something was haunting her. She said to herself, I can't go on like this, I must talk to somebody. Yet to whom and about what? What had she to complain of, other than the loneliness and boredom which was perfectly to be expected? Why was she suddenly now so frightened and sickened?

She saw ahead of her a small light moving in the darkness of the garden and she stopped in a fresh alarm. The light moved, questing, hesitating. It vanished for a moment and reappeared, a little round spot of light moving over foliage and stone. Marian decided that it must be an electric torch. She moved forward silently upon the gravel path, now grown so grassy and mossy that her feet made no sound. The light was a little to the right of the path, and the breathless girl had no thought but to glide quickly past it and then run in the direction of the house. Her heart fluttered violently and she increased her pace.

The light suddenly darted at her and she stopped in her tracks, seeing her feet, her dress, abruptly illumined. The gravel crunched under her heels. It was the first sound for a long time. The light moved up to her face and dazzled her and she gasped, caught.

"Miss Taylor."

●◆ In which story were you more of a participant? What did the author do to include you? What did the author do to make you more of an observer in the other story?

132

How does your stance as participant and observer affect the way you experience the unfolding events in the story? Consider the different effects achieved by each stance and how each serves different purposes. Be sure to use quotations from both passages to support your ideas.

133

Writers can make the reader a participant in or observer of the unfolding story.

Four

Then and Now

The ways in which a writer controls time in a story affects how you experience the unfolding events. As you read an excerpt from Anita Brookner's novel *Family and Friends*, notice how the narrator tells the story of Sofka and her family through several time frames.

← Response notes →

from *Family and Friends* by Anita Brookner

Here is Sofka, in a wedding photograph; at least, I assume it is a wedding, although the bride and groom are absent. Sofka stands straight and stern, her shoulders braced, her head erect in the manner of two generations earlier. She wears a beautiful beaded dress and an egret feather in her hair. It must have been attached to a hat but the hat is hidden by her coiffure, which is in itself hat-shaped. Behind her stand her two daughters, beautiful also, but looking curiously tubercular; perhaps those wide-eyed pleading smiles add to this impression. The daughters are in white, with ribbons in their long hair, which I know to have been red. Sofka's eldest son, her pride and joy, smiles easily, already a lazy conqueror. In his white tie and tails he has the air of an orchestral conductor. He stands between the two girls, an escort rather than a brother, as he was to prove on so many occasions. The sickly and favoured younger son is nowhere in sight, unless he proves to be one of those touching and doomed-looking children seated cross-legged in the front row, the girls, with hair of unimaginable length, clutching posies of flowers, the boys in long trousers and jackets of a satiny-looking material, gazing soulfully at the photographer. Yes, Alfred must be the one on the right. All around them are lesser members of the cast, relations by marriage: a stout and equally beaded woman, several jovial men, a youngish woman with a cascading jabot of lace and an expression of dedicated purpose, and, on the extreme left, edging her way into the centre, a pretty girl with a face like a bird. None of these people seems to have as much right to be in the picture as Sofka does. It is as if she has given birth to the entire brood, but having done so, thinks little of them. This I know to be the case. She gazes out of the photograph, beyond the solicitations of the photographer, her eyes remote and unsmiling, as if contemplating some unique destiny. Compared with her timeless expression, her daughters' pleading smiles already foretell their future. And those favoured sons, who clearly have their mother's blessing, there is something there too that courts disaster. Handsome Frederick, in his white tie and tails, with his orchestral conductor's panache: is there not perhaps something too easy about him, pliable, compliant, weak? Able to engage his mother's collusion in many an amorous escapade, but finally dishonourable, disappointing? Does Sofka already know this? And little Alfred, seated cross-legged between the children who must be sisters and with one of whom he will shortly fall in love, do those eyes, heavy and solemn, shadowed with the strain of behaving well, bear in them the portent of a life

from *Family and Friends* by Anita Brookner

←—Response notes—→

spent obeying orders, working hard, being a credit, being a consolation, being a balm for his mother's hurt, a companion in her isolation? For her husband, their father, is absent, gone before, dead, mildly disgraced. Gambling, they say. In any event, he was an older man, scarcely compatible, out of reach to his young children, amused by his young wife but easily bored by her inflexible dignity. Out of it in every sense.

And now I see that it is in fact a wedding photograph. The bride and groom were there all the time, in the centre, as they should be. A good-looking couple. But lifeless, figures from stock. Above the bridegroom's shoulder, standing on something, perhaps, Sofka gazes ahead, with her family's future before her. No one to touch her. As it proved.

I have no doubt that once the photograph was taken, and the wedding group dispersed, the festivities took their normal course. I have no doubt that great quantities of delicious food—things in aspic, things in baskets of spun sugar—were consumed, and that the music struck up and the bride and bridegroom danced, oblivious of their guests, and that the elders gathered in groups on their gilt chairs while the children, flushed with too many sweetmeats and the lure of the polished parquet floor, ventured forth until restrained by nurses or grandmothers. I have no doubt that as the evening wore on the cigar-scented reminiscences induced many an indulgent nod, a nostalgic smile never to be recovered in the harder commerce of daily life. I have no doubt that those anonymous and jovial men (husbands, of course) relaxed into the sweetness of this precarious harmony, having found at last what married life had seemed to promise them, and their golden smiles, their passive decent good natures, the sudden look of worldliness their faces assumed as their lips closed voluptuously round the fine Romeo y Julietas and they lifted their heads a little to expel the bluish smoke reminded their wives— censorious women, with higher standards—why they had married them. Sofka would be at the centre of this group, of any group. Handsome Frederick would be dancing, sweeping some girl off her feet, making suggestions which she would not dare take seriously, and perhaps neither would he, with his mother watching him. Later, perhaps, or so the girls would like to think. Little Alfred would manfully trundle his cousin round the floor, looking to his mother for approval, and in so doing lose both her approval and his own heart. The girls, Mireille and Babette (Mimi and Betty), would stay with their mother, waiting for her permission to dance. But the young men, faced with the prospect of negotiating for that permission, would not insist, and the girls would not dance much. Sofka gave out that the girls were delicate. And indeed they looked it.

I find it entirely appropriate and indeed characteristic that Sofka should have named her sons after kings and emperors and her daughters as if they were characters in a musical comedy. Thus were their roles designated for them. The boys were to conquer, and the girls to flirt.

135

Mark the different points in time referred to in the narration. Tell what each contributes to your overall understanding of the family's story.

1. Past of Two Generations Earlier

   Contribution:

   ....

   ....

   ....

2. Present when Wedding Photograph is Taken

   Contribution:

   ....

   ....

   ....

3. Future after Wedding

   Contribution:

   ....

   ....

   ....

4. Present of Narrator's Thoughts

   Contribution:

   ....

   ....

   ....

●◆ To explore how the use of time creates different experiences for the reader, write about the wedding from the point of view of one of Sofka's children. Write one paragraph in present tense—that is, during the actual wedding.

....

....

....

....

Writers make use of various time frames as a story unfolds to control how the reader will experience and participate in the story.

Five

Creating the Experience

Write an episode of your own. First think of an incident to tell. List the characters involved and highlight the major events in your story. Use at least two of the techniques examined in the first four lessons—anticipation, empathy, observer and participant roles, and multiple time frames—in order to involve your reader in the story.

Describe the incident:

Describe the characters:

137

Outline the events:

Techniques to help involve the reader:

●◆Now write the incident, keeping in mind that one of your purposes is to create the experience for your reader.

Using different techniques to heighten anticipation and empathy will help a reader experience the events of a story.

Language and Story

Language creates tone, it helps define theme, and it reveals characters. Certain writers go beyond the more common uses of language into something that could be termed "language play." The play is not an end in itself but is motivated by the writer's attempts to have fun with and explore the limits of language. What may seem nonsense is also "purposeful." Made-up language evokes different reactions and types of understanding from readers and is used to emphasize how language conveys more than the literal meaning of words. Analyze the way language works in a story and the words a writer chooses to express the feelings and actions of the story.

One Word Play

As a writer, Lewis Carroll explored the limits of language. His novels *Alice in Wonderland* and *Through the Looking-Glass* are extended examinations of words and playful ideas. At one point in *Through the Looking-Glass*, Alice happens upon a book lying on a table. Alice turns the pages trying to find something she can read, but it is in a language she does not understand. At last she realizes that it is a Looking-Glass book, and if she holds it up to a mirror, the words will "all go the right way again." She turns to the poem "Jabberwocky."

Response notes

Jabberwocky
Lewis Carroll

'Twas brillig, and the slithy toves
  Did gyre and gimble in the wabe:
All mimsy were the borogoves,
    And the mome raths outgrabe.

"Beware the Jabberwock, my son!
  The jaws that bite, the claws that catch!
Beware the Jubjub bird, and shun
    The frumious Bandersnatch!"

He took his vorpal sword in hand:
  Long time the manxome foe he sought—
So rested he by the Tumtum tree,
    And stood awhile in thought.

And, as in uffish thought he stood,
  The Jabberwock, with eyes of flame,
Came whiffling through the tulgey wood,
    And burbled as it came!

One, two! One, two! And through and through
  The vorpal blade went snicker-snack!
He left it dead, and with its head
    He went galumphing back.

"And hast thou slain the Jabberwock?
  Come to my arms, my beamish boy!
O frabjous day! Callooh! Callay!"
    He chortled in his joy.

'Twas brillig, and the slithy toves
  Did gyre and gimble in the wabe:
All mimsy were the borogoves,
    And the mome raths outgrabe.

During Alice's adventures, Humpty Dumpty explains to Alice that *slithy* combines *lithe* and *slimy* and that *frumious* combines *fuming* and *furious*. Make a glossary of ten key words that help explain your interpretation of the story behind the poem.

GLOSSARY

Word from Poem	Meanings
1.	
2.	
3.	
4.	
5.	
6.	
7.	
8.	
9.	
10.	

141

Imagine a scenario that might have given rise to this poem. Write a short description that tells who the poem is about and what happens. Include the setting and use some of the words you listed in the chart above.

The reader can construct the sense of a story without knowing the specific meaning of each word.

John Lennon was famous as a musician, but he also wrote stories. He wrote two books of what he called "Liverpudlian nonsense poems and stories"—writing that relied heavily on language play. They are the outcome of his fascination with the many **dialects** of Liverpool, the city where he grew up. Why play with language? Read Lennon's very short story, keeping that question in mind.

"Randolf's Party" by John Lennon

←—Response notes—→

It was Chrisbus time but Randolph was alone. Where were all his good pals. Bernie, Dave, Nicky, Alice, Beddy, Freba, Viggy, Nigel, Alfred, Clive, Stan, Frenk, Tom, Harry, George, Harold? Where were they on this day? Randolf looged saggly at his only Chrispbut cart from his dad who did not live there.

"I can't understan this being so aloneley on the one day of the year when one would surely spect a pal or two?" thought Rangolf. Hanyway he carried on putting ub the desicrations and muzzle toe. All of a surgeon there was amerry timble on the door. Who but who could be a knocking on my door? He opened it and there standing there who? but only his pals. Bernie, Dave, Nicky, Alice, Beddy, Freba, Viggy, Nigel, Alfred, Clive, Stan, Frenk, Tom, Harry, George, Harold weren't they?

Come on in old pals buddys and mates. With a big griff on his face Randoff welcombed them. In they came jorking and labbing shoubing "Haddy Grimmble, Randoob." and other hearty, and then they all jumbed on him and did smite him with mighty blows about his head crying, "We never liked you all the years we've known you. You were never raelly one of us you know, soft head."

They killed him you know, at least he didn't *die* alone did he? Merry Chrustchove, Randolf old pal buddy.

Talk with a partner about this story. Share ideas and questions from your annotations and summarize what you think happens in the story.

☞ What can you say about the narrator's **tone**—that is, his attitude toward Randolf and what happens to him? Complete the following statement: The narrator's attitude toward the situation and the character is

....

....

....

Words that are made up or that nearly resemble actual words can be an effective way to convey tone and meaning. In the case of Lennon's story, we take away at least some understanding of the narrator's attitude by the language he uses in telling the story.

In the chart below, list words or phrases that you think help convey the narrator's attitude toward Randolf and the events. For example, variations of actual words—"Chrisbus," "muzzle toe," "big griff on his face." Then explain the effect of these words on tone.

Words that Convey Tone	Attitude Conveyed
"looged saggly"	sees Randolph as

●❖ Write a brief episode of your own that relies heavily on made-up language to characterize your narrator's attitude toward the subject.

Writers sometimes create words for fun and effect. The words often characterize the narrator and reveal his or her tone toward the subject.

More often than not, writers use fairly standard language in their stories. When language falls outside the standard speech patterns and vocabulary that people use in their everyday lives, it may be difficult to understand. In *A Clockwork Orange*, Anthony Burgess created a futuristic world. A fifteen-year-old "droog," Alex, narrates the novel through an invented **slang**. As you read, keep track of your questions about this language and the problems you have understanding it.

←—*Response notes*—→

from *A Clockwork Orange* by Anthony Burgess

"Hi hi hi, there. A lot better after the day's rest. Ready now for evening work to earn that little bit." For that's what they said they believed I did these days. "Yum yum, mum. Any of that for me?" It was like some frozen pie that she'd unfroze and then warmed up and it looked not so very appetitish, but I had to say what I said. Dad looked at me with a not-so-pleased suspicious like look but said nothing, knowing he dared not, and mum gave me a tired like little smeck, to thee fruit of my womb my only son sort of. I danced to the bathroom and had a real skory cheest all over, feeling dirty and gluey, then back to my den for the evening's platties. Then, shining, combed, brushed and gorgeous, I sat to my lomtick of pie. Papapa said:

"Not that I want to pry, son, but where exactly is it you go to work of evenings?"

"Oh," I chewed, "it's mostly odd things, helping like. Here and there, as it might be." I gave him a straight dirty glazzy, as to say to mind his own and I'd mind mine. "I never ask for money, do I? Not money for clothes or for pleasures? All right, then, why ask?"

My dad was like humble mumble chumble. "Sorry, son," he said. "But I get worried sometimes. Sometimes I have dreams. You can laugh if you like, but there's a lot in dreams. Last night I had this dream with you in it and I didn't like it one bit."

"Oh?" He had gotten me interessovatted now, dreaming of me like that. I had like a feeling I had had a dream, too, but I could not remember proper what. "Yes?" I said, stopping chewing my gluey pie.

"It was vivid," said my dad. "I saw you lying on the street and you had been beaten by other boys. These boys were like the boys you used to go around with before you were sent to that last Corrective School."

"Oh?" I had an in-grin at that, papapa believing I had real reformed or believing he believed. And then I remembered my own dream, which was a dream of that morning, of Georgie giving his general's orders and old Dim smecking around toothless as he wielded the whip. But dreams go by opposites I was once told. "Never worry about thine only son and heir, O my father," I said. "Fear not. He canst taketh care of himself, verily."

"And," said my dad, "you were like helpless in your blood and you couldn't fight back." That was real opposites, so I had another quiet from *A Clockwork Orange* by Anthony Burgess

malenky grin within and then I took all the deng out of my carmans and tinkled it on the saucy table-cloth. I said:

"Here, dad, it's not much. It's what I earned last night. But perhaps for the odd peet of Scotchman in the snug somewhere for you and mum."

"Thanks, son," he said. "But we don't go out much now. We daren't go out much, the streets being what they are. Young hooligans and so on. Still, thanks. I'll bring her home a bottle of something tomorrow." And he scooped this ill-gotten pretty into his trouser carmans, mum being at the cheesting of the dishes in the kitchen. And I went out with loving smiles all round.

← Response notes →

●◆ A way to understand the invented language is to use a method called *sub-texting*. In sub-texting your job is to translate each sentence. Read the paragraphs of Alex's story that follow. Under the original, write your translation.

When I got to the bottom of the stairs of the flatblock I was somewhat surprised. I was more

....

than that. I opened my rot like wide in the old stony gapes. They had come to meet me. They were

....

145

waiting by the all scrawled-over municipal wall-painting of the nagoy dignity of labour, bare vecks

....

and cheenas stern at the wheels of industry, like I said, with all this dirt pencilled from their rots

....

by naughty malchicks. Dim had a big thick like stick of black greasepaint and was tracing filthy

....

slovos real big over our municipal painting and doing the old Dim guff—wuh huh huh—while he did

....

it. But he turned round when Georgie and Pete gave me the well hello, showing their shining

....

droogy zoobies, and he horned out: "He are here, he have arrived, horray," and did a clumsy

....

turnitoe bit of dancing.

....

With a partner, compare translations and discuss what helped guide the decisions about meaning.

Use various strategies— rereading, discussing, questioning, and sub-texting— as ways to make difficult language more accessible.

Four Language and Characterization

Writers use language to emphasize physical and personality traits of a character. A character's language defines him. In *A Clockwork Orange*, we learn about Alex through how he talks and the ways in which he expresses his understanding of the world around him. What does the invented slang reveal about him and the world in which he lives? The following passage is a continuation of the earlier episode.

from ***A Clockwork Orange*** by Anthony Burgess

← *Response notes* →

"Appy polly loggies," I said, careful. "I had something of a pain in the gulliver so had to sleep. I was not wakened when I gave orders for wakening. Still, here we all are, ready for what the old nochy offers, yes?" I seemed to have picked up that yes? from P. R. Deltoid, my Post-Corrective Adviser. Very strange.

"Sorry about the pain," said Georgie, like very concerned. "Using the gulliver too much like, maybe. Giving orders and discipline and such, perhaps. Sure the pain is gone? Sure you'll not be happier going back to the bed?" And they all had a bit of a malenky grin.

"Wait," I said. "Let's get things nice and sparkling clear. This sarcasm, if I may call it such, does not become you, O my little friends. Perhaps you have been having a bit of a quiet govoreet behind my back, making your own little jokes and such-like. As I am your droog and leader, surely I am entitled to know what goes on, eh? Now then, Dim, what does that great big horsy gape of a grin portend?" For Dim had his rot open in a sort of bezoomny soundless smeck. Georgie got in very skorry with:

"All right, no more picking on Dim, brother. That's part of the new way."

"New way?" I said. "What's this about a new way? There's been some very large talk behind my sleeping back and no error. Let me slooshy more." And I sort of folded my rookers and leaned comfortable to listen against the broken banister-rail, me being still higher than them, droogs as they called themselves, on the third stair.

"No offence, Alex," said Pete, "but we wanted to have things more democratic like. Not like you like saying what to do and what not all the time. But no offence." Georgie said:

"Offence is neither here nor elsewhere. It's a matter of who has ideas. What ideas has he had? And he kept his very bold glazzies turned full on me. "It's all the small stuff, malenky veshches like last night. We're growing up, brothers."

"More," I said, not moving. "Let me slooshy more."

"Well," said Georgie, "if you must have it, have it then. We itty round, shop-crasting and the like, coming out with a pitiful rookerful of cutter each. And there's Will the English and the Muscleman coffee mesto saying he can fence anything that any malchick cares to try to crast. The shiny stuff, the ice," he said, still with these like cold glazzies on me. "The big big big money is available is what Will the English says."

146

from ***A Clockwork Orange*** by Anthony Burgess

← Response notes →

"So," I said very comfortable out but real razdraz within. "Since when have you been consorting and comporting with Will the English?"

"Now and again," said George, "I get around all on my oddy knocky. Like last Sabbath for instance. I can live my own jeezny, droogie, right?"

I didn't really care for any of this, my brothers. "And what will you do," I said, "with the big big big deng or money as you so highfaluting call it? Have you not every veshch you need? If you need an auto you pluck it from the trees. If you need pretty polly you take it. Yes? Why this sudden shilarny for being the big bloated capitalist?"

"Ah," said Georgie, "you think and govoreet sometimes like a little child." Dim went huh huh huh at that. "Tonight," said Georgie, "we pull a mansize crast."

So my dream had told truth, then. Georgie the general saying what we should do and what not do, Dim with the ship as mindless grinning bulldog. But I played with care, with great care, the greatest, saying, smiling: "Good. Real horrorshow. Initiative comes to them as wait. I have taught you much, little droogie. Now tell me what you have in mind, Georgieboy."

"Oh," said Georgie, cunning and crafty in his grin, "the old moloko-plus first, would you not say? Something to sharpen us up, boy, but you especially, we having the start of you."

"You have govoreeted my thoughts for me," I smiled away. "I was about to suggest the dear old Korova. Good good good. Lead, little Georgie." And I made with a like deep bow, smiling like bezoomny but thinking all the time. But when we got into the street I viddied that thinking is for the gloopy ones and that the oomny ones use like inspiration and what Bog sends. For now it was lovely music that came to my aid. There was an auto ittying by and it had its radio on, and I could just slooshy a bar or so of Ludwig van (it was the Violin Concerto, last movement), and I viddied right at once what to do. I said, in like a thick deep goloss: "Right, Georgie, now," and I whished out my cut-throat britva. Georgie said: "Uh?" but he was skorry enough with his nozh, the blade coming sloosh out of the handle, and we were on to each other. Old Dim said: "Oh, no, not right that isn't," and made to uncoil the chain round his tally, but Pete said, putting his rooker firm on old Dim: "Leave them. It's right like that." So then Georgie and Your Humble did the old quiet catstalk, looking for openings, knowing each other's style a bit too horrorshow really, Georgie now and then going lurch lurch with his shining nozh but not no wise connecting. And all the time lewdies passed by and viddied all this but minded their own, it being perhaps a common street-sight.

147

What is going on here? Talk with a partner about your questions and reactions.

●◆ Now examine how the language characterizes the narrator and his friends. Write five statements about Alex, his family, and friends. Then find a quotation or two from the story to support your assertion.

Assertion: *Alex is philosophical.*

Quote: *"You can viddy that everything in this wicked world counts."*

"You can pony that one thing always lead to another."

Assertion #1:

Quote:

Assertion #2:

Quote:

Assertion #3:

Quote:

Assertion #4:

Quote:

Assertion #5:

Quote:

> Writers use invented language to help reveal their characters' traits and qualities.

Five Creating Meaning Through Language

How would you use language to achieve certain effects in a story? In the following chart, brainstorm ideas for a story of your own that relies on language play to emphasize meaning. Begin by determining a plot for your story. Determine what characteristics of language play will emphasize the story's meaning. Then, decide on a narrator who will provide the perspective on events. Let your imagination go and use language to create the meaning of this event.

Ideas for a story:

Characteristics of language play to emphasize meaning:

Narrator's perspective:

A few sentences from the narrator's perspective:

●◆Once the chart is complete, begin drafting your story using language that intensifies the meaning. Use what you have learned about language from Carroll, Lennon, and Burgess as you write.

Experimenting with language for yourself is another way to understand the effects of language play on meaning.

Text and Context

If a friend says to you, "Go fly a kite," what do you think he means? You may hear it as another way of saying "I don't like that idea." If he is really angry with you, you might hear it as a challenge to fight. If you hear a small child say "Go fly a kite," it might be a request on a windy day. The same four words change meaning depending on the speaker, the speaker's feelings, and the circumstances.

Words have many meanings in literature too. One layer of meaning consists of the actual words on the page and the sense you make of them. Another layer of meaning is provided by the various contexts that affect the work. Knowing the context of a work of literature enriches your understanding of the text. While you can certainly interpret the words on the page without any background knowledge, considering the context will provide you with additional meanings. Context includes allusions to earlier works, geography, personal experience, political conditions, historical events, and so forth.

The meaning of a single statement may change, depending on the way the author uses it. This idea is at the heart of literary **allusions**—references to earlier works of literature. Look at the Latin phrase below. It is from an **ode** by the ancient Roman poet Horace.

> Dulce et decorum est pro patria mori.
> [It is sweet and honorable to die for one's country.]

What is the meaning for Horace? What emotion is he describing?

Now, read a poem that uses part of that statement for the title. In World War I, after gas was introduced as a weapon, gas masks were distributed. They could save a soldier's life—if they were used in time. The "Five-Nines" referred to in line eight were artillery shells.

Response notes

Dulce et Decorum Est
Wilfred Owen

Bent double, like old beggars under sacks,
Knock-kneed, coughing like hags, we cursed through sludge,
Till on the haunting flares we turned our backs
And toward our distant rest began to trudge.
Men marched asleep. Many had lost their boots
But limped on, blood-shod. All went lame; all blind;
Drunk with fatigue; deaf even to the hoots
Of tired, outstripped Five-Nines that dropped behind.

Gas! GAS! Quick, boys!—An ecstasy of fumbling,
Fitting the clumsy helmets just in time;
But someone still was yelling out and stumbling
And flound'ring like a man in fire or lime . . .
Dim, through the misty panes and thick green light,
As under a green sea, I saw him drowning.

In all my dreams, before my helpless sight,
He plunges at me, guttering, choking, drowning.

If in some smothering dreams you too could pace
Behind the wagon that we flung him in,
And watch the white eyes writhing in his face,
His hanging face, like a devil's sick of sin;
If you could hear, at every jolt, the blood
Come gargling from the froth-corrupted lungs,
Obscene as cancer, bitter as the cud
Of vile, incurable sores on innocent tongues,—
My friend, you would not tell with such high zest
To children ardent for some desperate glory,
The old Lie: *Dulce et decorum est*
Pro patria mori.

●◆ The speaker expresses powerful emotions. Take a few minutes to jot down your initial reactions to this poem and to the way that Owen uses Horace's line.

....

....

....

....

Wilfred Owen was an idealistic young man of twenty-one when World War I broke out in 1914. He enlisted and fought in France. He spent more than a year hospitalized after a nervous collapse before returning to the front where he was killed in action—one week before the Armistice of 1918. Return to the poem and underline five striking details that demonstrate to Owen that Horace's phrase is an "old Lie."

●◆ Using the details you identified, and others as necessary, write a letter from Owen to his family in 1918, soon after he returns to fighting. In your letter, try to put yourself in the poet's place as he describes how disillusioned he is by the reality of war.

153

....

....

....

....

....

....

....

....

....

....

....

....

....

....

Active reading requires understanding how the context of an allusion can change the meaning.

The Irish poet Patrick Kavanagh was influential in encouraging Irish poets to focus on the details of their surroundings. He wrote: "To know fully even one field or one lane is a lifetime's experience. In the world of poetic experience it is depth that counts and not width. A gap in a hedge, a smooth rock surfacing a narrow lane, a view of a woody meadow, the stream at the junction of four small fields—these are as much as a man can fully experience." Consider whether or not you agree with him as you read "The Reading Lesson."

Response notes

The Reading Lesson
Richard Murphy

Fourteen years old, learning the alphabet,
He finds letters harder to catch than hares
Without a greyhound. Can't I give him a dog
To track them down, or put them in a cage?
He's caught in a trap, until I let him go,
Pinioned by "Don't you want to learn to read?"
"I'll be the same man whatever I do."

He looks at a page as a mule balks at a gap
From which a goat may hobble out and bleat.
His eyes jink from a sentence like flushed snipe
Escaping shot. A sharp word, and he'll mooch
Back to his piebald mare and bantam cock.
Our purpose is as tricky to retrieve
As mercury from a smashed thermometer.

"I'll not read anymore." Should I give up?
His hands, long-fingered as a Celtic scribe's,
Will grow callous, gathering sticks or scrap;
Exploring pockets of the horny drunk
Loiterers at the fairs, giving them lice.
A neighbor chuckles. "You can never tame
The wild duck: when his wings grow, he'll fly off."

If books resembled roads, he'd quickly read:
But they're small farms to him, fenced by the page,
Ploughed into lines, with letters drilled like oats:
A field of tasks he'll always be outside.
If words were bank-notes, he would filch a wad;
If they were pheasants, they'd be in his pot
For breakfast, or if wrens he'd make them king.

154

Murphy gives you many details of the place where the speaker, the boy, and the neighbor live. To visualize the scene more fully, in the response notes sketch the place Murphy is describing.

How do the local details help you get an impression of the boy who is learning to read? To answer this question, rewrite the last stanza. Use details from a setting that you are familiar with or from one that you can imagine in sufficient detail. Fill in the blanks in the stanza that follows.

If books resembled _____, he'd quickly read: But they're_____

_____ to him, _____ by the page,_____

_____ into lines, with letters _____ like _____:

A _____ of tasks he'll always be outside.

If words were _____, he would _____;

If they were _____, they'd be _____

_____, or if _____ he'd make them king.

●◆ Now, write a short paragraph explaining how the context of place affects the image you get of the boy.

The geography of a place can shape your view of events and characters in a literary work.

Shifting Personal Perspectives

Do you remember the first time you saw a particular place as a child? If you returned to it years later, did it seem different? Perhaps the formerly towering trees seemed smaller? Or you realized that the noises that scared you as a child were just normal, everyday sounds? With age and experience, the view we have of a thing changes. Jamaica Kincaid was born in 1949 in Antigua, at that time a British colony. What is her perspective of England?

"On Seeing England for the First Time" by Jamaica Kincaid

←—*Response notes*—→

When I saw England for the first time, I was a child in school sitting at a desk. The England I was looking at was laid out on a map gently, beautifully, delicately, a very special jewel; it lay on a bed of sky blue—the background of the map—its yellow form mysterious, because though it looked like a leg of mutton, it could not really look like anything so familiar as a leg of mutton because it was England— with shadings of pink and green, unlike any shadings of pink and green I had seen before, squiggly veins of red running in every direction. England was a special jewel all right, and only special people got to wear it. The people who got to wear England were English people. They wore it well and they wore it everywhere: in jungles, in deserts, on plains, on top of the highest mountains, on all the oceans, on all the seas. When my teacher had pinned this map up on the blackboard, she said, "This is England"—and she said it with authority, seriousness, and adoration, and we all sat up. It was as if she had said, "This is Jerusalem, the place you will go to when you die but only if you have been good." We understood then—we were meant to understand then—that England was to be our source of myth and the source from which we got our sense of reality, our sense of what was meaningful, our sense of what was meaningless—and much about our own lives and much about the very idea of us headed that last list.

At the time I was a child sitting at my desk seeing England for the first time, I was already very familiar with the greatness of it. Each morning before I left for school, I ate a breakfast of half a grapefruit, an egg, bread and butter and a slice of cheese, and a cup of cocoa; or half a grapefruit, a bowl of oat porridge, bread and butter and a slice of cheese, and a cup of cocoa. The can of cocoa was often left on the table in front of me. It had written on it the name of the company, the year the company was established, and the words "Made in England." Those words, "Made in England," were written on the box the oats came in too. They would also have been written on the box the shoes I was wearing came in; the bolt of gray linen cloth lying on the shelf of a store from which my mother had bought three yards to make the uniform that I was wearing had written along its edge those three words. The shoes I wore were made in England; so were my socks and cotton undergarments and the satin ribbons I wore tied at the end of two plaits of my hair. My father, who might have sat next

"On Seeing England for the First Time" by Jamaica Kincaid

←— Response notes —→

to me at breakfast, was a carpenter and cabinetmaker. The shoes he wore to work would have been made in England, as were his khaki shirt and trousers, his underpants and undershirt, his socks and brown felt hat. Felt was not the proper material from which a hat that was expected to provide shade from the hot sun should have been made, but my father must have seen and admired a picture of an Englishman wearing such a hat in England, and this picture that he saw must have been so compelling that it caused him to wear the wrong hat for a hot climate most of his long life. And this hat—a brown felt hat—became so central to his character that it was the first thing he put on in the morning as he stepped out of bed and the last thing he took off before he stepped back into bed at night. As we sat at breakfast, a car might go by. The car, a Hillman or a Zephyr, was made in England. The very idea of the meal itself, breakfast, and its substantial quality and quantity, was an idea from England; we somehow knew that in England they began the day with this meal called breakfast, and a proper breakfast was a big breakfast. No one I knew liked eating so much food so early in the day; it made us feel sleepy, tired. But this breakfast business was "Made in England" like almost everything else that surrounded us, the exceptions being the sea, the sky, and the air we breathed.

At the time I saw this map—seeing England for the first time—I did not say to myself, "Ah, so that's what it looks like," because there was no longing in me to put a shape to those three words that ran through every part of my life no matter how small; for me to have had such a longing would have meant that I lived in a certain atmosphere, an atmosphere in which those three words were felt as a burden. But I did not live in such an atmosphere. When my teacher showed us the map, she asked us to study it carefully, because no test we would ever take would be complete without this statement: "Draw a map of England." I did not know then that the statement "Draw a map of England" was something far worse than a declaration of war, for a flat-out declaration of war would have put me on alert. In fact, there was no need for war—I had long ago been conquered. I did not know then that this statement was part of a process that would result in my erasure—not my physical erasure, but my erasure all the same. I did not know then that this statement was meant to make me feel awe and small whenever I heard the word "England": awe at the power of its existence, small because I was not from it.

After that there were many times of seeing England for the first time. I saw England in history. I knew the names of all the kings of England. I knew the names of their children, their wives, their disappointments, their triumphs, the names of people who betrayed them. I knew the dates on which they were born and the dates they died. I knew their conquests and was made to feel good if I figured in them; I knew their defeats.

Kincaid is recreating feelings she had as a child. There are several places in the essay where her adult perspective enters and expresses her contradictory feelings about England. Mark at least three of these places in the text.

●◆Focus on Kincaid's perspective as a child. Write a story or poem entitled "I See England" from the perspective of an elementary school student who has never been to England. You will need to imagine some of the details; be sure they are consistent with the details Kincaid presents.

Memory of personal experiences can provide one perspective on events and ideas. Active readers must understand that the writer's perspective shifts when writing about memories.

The Context of Politics

The relationship between a powerful country and its colonies is not always congenial. You may have already sensed that Jamaica Kincaid felt uncomfortable about being a colonial. Read the rest of her essay to understand the role that this political situation played in the intensity of her feelings.

"On Seeing England for the First Time" (continued)
by Jamaica Kincaid

← Response notes →

This view—the naming of the kings, their deeds, their disappointments —was the vivid view, the forceful view. There were other views, subtler ones, softer, almost not there—but these softer views were the ones that made the most lasting impression on me, the ones that made me really feel like nothing. "When morning touched the sky" was one phrase, for no morning touched the sky where I lived. The morning where I lived came on abruptly, with a shock of heat and loud noises. "Evening approaches" was another. But the evenings where I lived did not approach; in fact, I had no evening—I had night and I had day, and they came and went in a mechanical way: on, off, on, off. And then there were gentle mountains and low blue skies and moors over which people took walks for nothing but pleasure, when where I lived a walk was an act of labor, a burden, something only death or the automobile could relieve. And the weather there was so remarkable because the rain fell gently always, and the wind blew in gusts that were sometimes deep, and the air was various shades of gray, each an appealing shade for a dress to be worn when a portrait was being painted; and when it rained at twilight, wonderful things happened: People bumped into each other unexpectedly and that would lead to all sorts of turns of events—a plot, the mere weather caused plots.

The reality of my life, the life I led at the time I was being shown these views of England for the first time, for the second time, for the one hundred millionth time, was this: The sun shone with what sometimes seemed to be a deliberate cruelty; we must have done something to deserve that. My dresses did not rustle in the evening air as I strolled to the theater (I had no evening, I had no theater; my dresses were made of a cheap cotton, the weave of which would give way after not too many washings). I got up in the morning, I did my chores (fetched water from the public pipe for my mother, swept the yard), I washed myself, I went to a woman to have my hair combed freshly every day (because before we were allowed into our classroom our teachers would inspect us, and children who had not bathed that day, or had dirt under their fingernails, or whose hair had not been combed anew that day might not be allowed to attend class). I ate that breakfast. I walked to school. At school we gathered in an auditorium and sang a hymn, "All Things Bright and Beautiful," and looking down on us as we sang were portraits of the queen of England and her husband; they wore jewels and medals and they smiled. I was a Brownie. At each meeting we would form a little group around a flagpole, and after raising the Union Jack, we would say, "I promise to do my best, to do my duty to God and the queen, to help other people

159

every day and obey the scouts' law."

But who were these people and why had I never seen them? I
mean, really seen them, in the place where they lived? I had never
been to England. England! I had seen England's representatives. I had
seen the governor-general at the public grounds at a ceremony
celebrating the queen's birthday. I had seen an old princess and I had
seen a young princess. They had both been extremely not beautiful,
but who among us would have told them that? I had never seen
England, really seen it. I had only met a representative, seen a
picture, read books, memorized its history. I had never set foot, my
own foot, in it.

The space between the idea of something and its reality is always
wide and deep and dark. The longer they are kept apart—idea of
thing, reality of thing—the wider the width, the deeper the depth, the
thicker and darker the darkness. This space starts out empty, there is
nothing in it, but it rapidly becomes filled up with obsession or desire
or hatred or love—sometimes all of these things, sometimes some of
these things. That the idea of something and its reality are often two
completely different things is something no one ever remembers; and
so when they meet and find that they are not compatible, the weaker
of the two, idea or reality, dies.

And so finally, when I was a grown-up woman, the mother of two
children, the wife of someone, a person who resides in a powerful
country that takes up more than its fair share of a continent, the
owner of a house with many rooms in it and of two automobiles, with
the desire and will (which I very much act upon) to take from the
world more than I give back to it, more than I deserve, more than I
need, finally then, I saw England, the real England, not a picture, not
a painting, not through a story in a book, but England, for the first
time. In me, the space between the idea of it and its reality had
become filled with hatred, and so when at last I saw it I wanted to
take it into my hands and tear it into little pieces and then crumble it
up as if it were clay, child's clay. That was impossible, and so I could
only indulge in not-favorable opinions.

If I had told an English person what I thought, that I find England
ugly, that I hate England; the weather is like a jail sentence; the
English are a very ugly people; the food in England is like a jail
sentence; the hair of English people is so straight, so dead-looking; the
English have an unbearable smell so different from the smell of
people I know, real people, of course, I would have been told that I
was a person full of prejudice. Apart from the fact that it is I—that is,
the people who look like me—who would make that English person
aware of the unpleasantness of such a thing, the idea of such a thing,
prejudice, that person would have been only partly right, sort of right:
I may be capable of prejudice, but my prejudices have no weight to
them, my prejudices have no force behind them, my prejudices remain
opinions, my prejudices remain my personal opinion. And a great
feeling of rage and disappointment came over me as I looked at
England, my head full of personal opinions that could not have public,

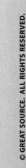

"On Seeing England for the First Time" by Jamaica Kincaid

←—Response notes—→

my public, approval. The people I come from are powerless to do evil on a grand scale.

The moment I wished every sentence, everything I knew, that began with England would end with "and then it all died, we don't know how, it just all died" was when I saw the white cliffs of Dover. I had sung hymns and recited poems that were about a longing to see the white cliffs of Dover again. At the time I sang the hymns and recited the poems, I could really long to see them again because I had never seen them at all, nor had anyone around me at the time. But there we were, groups of people longing for something we had never seen. And so there they were, the white cliffs, but they were not that pearly, majestic thing I used to sing about, that thing that created such a feeling in these people that when they died in the place where I lived they had themselves buried facing a direction that would allow them to see the white cliffs of Dover when they were resurrected, as surely they would be. The white cliffs of Dover, when finally I saw them, were cliffs, but they were not white; you could only call them that if the word "white" meant something special to you; they were steep; they were so steep, the correct height from which all my views of England, starting with the map before me in my classroom and ending with the trip I had just taken, should jump and die and disappear forever.

●◆Kincaid writes that the "space between the idea of something and its reality is always wide and deep and dark." She continues by writing that "when they meet and find that they are not compatible, the weaker of the two, idea or reality, dies." When she saw the white cliffs of Dover, what happened to her views of England? Reread the final paragraph of her essay and explain what happened when the idea and the reality met.

Politics can play an important role in developing a writer's perspective. The reader's understanding of a writer's feelings comes from the text itself and from knowing the political context.

Writers often expect readers to know the context of a work. They do not provide explicit details about time and place but instead suggest the context in subtle ways. You can understand the following poem on one level without considering the context. However, knowing about the events in Ireland in 1972 will increase your understanding.

Ireland 1972
Paul Durcan

Next to the fresh grave of my beloved grandmother
The grave of my firstlove murdered by my brother.

Response notes

1972 was the bloodiest year of the conflict in Northern Ireland, with people killed in bombings, reprisals, army shootings, and rioting. Durcan has focused his poem on the horrors of the long terrorist war there and its devastating effects on families.

How does knowing about what happened in Northern Ireland in 1972 change your understanding of the poem?

....

....

....

Write an original poem using this one as a model. Use a specific historical event as your context and subject. Include any details that are relevant in the title.

....

....

....

....

....

....

....

> Multiple contexts can shape the writer's work. Considering several perspectives on the text can enrich your understanding of the author's message.

Interpreting Nonfiction

Is it true?" "Did this really happen?" You have probably wondered about how factual a certain story or essay was. We generally expect nonfiction—essays, memoirs, journalism—to be more fact than fiction. However, you should not confuse factual content with objectivity. Writers of nonfiction reveal a definite point of view on their subject. They develop arguments in ways that will convince the reader. The writer also selects and arranges the details of the writing to present a unified whole. The final picture is a combination of observable facts and the writer's interpretation of them.

You need to identify the author's perspective so that you can evaluate facts and interpretations. You need to understand how an author develops his or her subject through word choice and structure. And you need to be able to understand and critique the author's arguments. In short, you must develop several perspectives for interpreting nonfiction.

One kind of nonfiction that requires careful reading is reporting. Journalism contains a combination of facts and interpretations. Some reporters keep themselves entirely removed from the events, while others actively participate in them. Analyzing the degree of **subjectivity** and the **point of view** of the author will help you interpret journalistic writing.

British writer Rebecca West was a strong advocate of social justice. After World War II, she wrote three articles about the trials of Nazi leaders in Nuremberg. The first one was written in 1946, in the eleventh month of the trials. Think about how her attitude toward the Nazi leaders is revealed in her descriptions.

← Response notes →

from "Greenhouse with Cyclamens—I" by Rebecca West

There rushed up towards the plane the astonishing face of the world's enemy: pinewoods on little hills, grey-green glossy lakes, too small ever to be anything but smooth, gardens tall with red-tongued beans, fields striped with copper wheat, russet-roofed villages with headlong gables and pumpkin-steeple churches that no architect over seven could have designed. Another minute and the plane dropped to the heart of the world's enemy: Nuremberg. It took not many more minutes to get to the courtroom where the world's enemy was being tried for his sins; but immediately those sins were forgotten in wonder at a conflict which was going on in that court, though it had nothing to do with the indictments considered by it. The trial was then in its eleventh month, and the courtroom was a citadel of boredom. Every person within its walk was in the grip of extreme tedium. This is not to say that the work in hand was being performed languidly. An iron discipline met that tedium head on and did not yield an inch to it. But all the same the most spectacular process in the court was by then a certain tug-of-war concerning time. Some of those present were fiercely desiring that that tedium should come to an end at the first possible moment, and the others were as fiercely desiring that it should last for ever and ever.

The people in court who wanted the tedium to endure eternally were the twenty-one defendants in the dock: who disconcerted the spectator by presenting the blatant appearance that historical characters, particularly in distress, assume in bad pictures. They looked what they were as crudely as Mary Queen of Scots at Fotheringay or Napoleon on St. Helena in a mid-Victorian Academy success. But it was, of course, an unusually ghastly picture. They were wreathed in suggestions of death. Not only were they in peril of the death sentence, there was constant talk about millions of dead and arguments whether these had died because of these men or not; knowing so well what death is, and experiencing it by anticipation, these men preferred the monotony of the trial to its cessation. So they clung on to the procedure through their lawyers and stretched it to the limits of its texture; and thus they aroused in the rest of the

164

from **"Greenhouse with Cyclamens—I"** by Rebecca West

court, the people who had a prospect of leaving Nuremberg and going back to life, a savage impatience. This the iron discipline of the court prevented from finding an expression for itself. But it made the air more tense.

It seemed ridiculous for the defendants to make any effort to stave off the end, for they admitted by their appearance that nothing was to go well with them again on this earth. These Nazi leaders, self-dedicated to the breaking of all rules, broke last of all the rule that the verdict of a court must not be foretold. Their appearance announced what they believed. The Russians had asked for the death penalty for all of them, and it was plain that the defendants thought that wish would be granted. Believing that they were to lose everything, they forgot what possession had been. Not the slightest trace of their power and their glory remained, none of them looked as if he could ever have exercised any valid authority. Goering still used imperial gestures, but they were so vulgar that they did not suggest that he had really filled any great position, it merely seemed probable that in certain bars the frequenters had called him by some such nickname as "The Emperor." These people were also surrendering physical characteristics which might have been thought inalienable during life, such as the colour and texture of their skins and the moulding of their features. Most of them, except Schacht, who was white-haired, and Speer, who was black like a monkey, were neither dark nor fair any more; and there was amongst them no leanness that did not sag and no plumpness that seemed more than inflation by some thin gas. So diminished were their personalities that it was hard to keep in mind which was which, even after one had sat and looked at them for days; and those who stood out defined themselves by oddity rather than character.

Hess was noticeable because he was so plainly mad: so plainly mad that it seemed shameful that he should be tried. His skin was ashen and he had that odd faculty, peculiar to lunatics, of falling into strained positions which no normal person could maintain for more than a few minutes, and staying fixed in contortion for hours. He had the classless air characteristic of asylum inmates; evidently his distracted personality had torn up all clues to his past. He looked as if his mind had no surface, as if every part of it had been blasted away except the depth where the nightmares live. Schacht was as noticeable because he was so far from mad, so completely his ordinary self in these extraordinary circumstances. He sat twisted in his seat so that his tall body, stiff as a plank, was propped against the end of the dock, which ought to have been at his side. Thus he sat at right angles to his fellow-defendants and looked past them and over their heads: it was always his argument that he was far superior to Hitler's gang. Thus, too, he sat at right angles to the judges on the bench confronting him: it was his argument too that he was a leading international banker, a most respectable man, and no court on earth could have the right to try him. He was petrified by rage because this court was pretending to have this right. He might have been a corpse

from **"Greenhouse with Cyclamens—I"** by Rebecca West

frozen by rigor mortis, a disagreeable corpse who had contrived to aggravate the process so that he should be specially difficult to fit into his coffin.

A few others were still individuals. Streicher was pitiable, because it was plainly the community and not he who was guilty of his sins. He was a dirty old man of the sort that gives trouble in parks, and a sane Germany would have sent him to an asylum long before. Baldur von Schirach, the Youth Leader, startled because he was like a woman in a way not common among men who looked like women. It was as if a neat and mousy governess sat there, not pretty, but with never a hair out of place, and always to be trusted never to intrude when there were visitors: as it might be Jane Eyre. And though one had read surprising news of Goering for years, he still surprised. He was so very soft. Sometimes he wore a German air-force uniform, and sometimes a light beach suit in the worst of playful taste, and both hung loosely on him, giving him an air of pregnancy. He had thick, brown young hair, the coarse bright skin of an actor who has used grease-paint for decades, and the preternaturally deep wrinkles of the drug-addict. It added up to something like the head of a ventriloquist's dummy. He looked infinitely corrupt, and acted naively.

Circle the number below that you think describes West's degree of objectivity or subjectivity.

Very Objective   Very Subjective
    1   2   3   4   5

What is it in West's writing that gave you the impression you indicated? Write a few sentences defending your opinion.

A writer's perspective often determines what facts are selected and how they are presented.

Two Aspects of the Subject

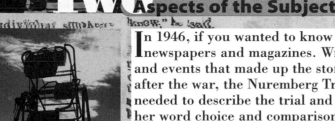

In 1946, if you wanted to know the news, you had to listen to the radio or read newspapers and magazines. Writers had to make readers actually see the people and events that made up the story. Because of a shortage of newsprint during and after the war, the Nuremberg Trials had not been covered in detail. Rebecca West needed to describe the trial and the defendants in detail for her readers. Therefore, her word choice and comparisons are especially significant. Note how she uses them to develop three major aspects of the subject: death, madness, and the loss of power.

Reread the excerpt from "Greenhouse with Cyclamens—I" and analyze the language West uses. Fill in the chart with words, phrases, and comparisons from the text for each category.

Death	Madness	Loss of power and glory
Schacht might have been "a corpse frozen by rigor mortis."	Hess was "classless" and "distracted."	So diminished were their personalities that it "was hard to keep in mind which was which . . . ."

To understand better how West's **diction** helps her compose pictures of the defendants, in the cluster below compose your own picture of a famous person that you do not admire. Decide which characteristic you want to emphasize about that person. Write it in the center circle. Then add related words, phrases, and comparisons in the remaining circles.

168

Understanding an Opinion

Rebecca West's observations of the Nuremberg trials reveal her **opinions** about the dark and light sides of human nature. Through her reports, she commented on larger topics such as good and evil, justice and injustice. As you read another excerpt from "Greenhouse with Cyclamens—I," think about the technique she used to reveal her opinion about the events.

from "Greenhouse with Cyclamens—I" by Rebecca West

←—Response notes —→

The system, with all its failures, got the travellers to Nuremberg in good time. At once a split appeared between those who had come to the trial for, say, the opening and these last two days, and those who had a longer experience of the sessions. The court had issued a directive that no photographs were to be taken of the defendants at the times when they were being sentenced. This seemed to some journalists who had just arrived a shocking interference with the rights of the press, and even some historians thought that it would leave the film record of the case regrettably incomplete. But those who had frequented the court over months were for the most part of a different mind.

The issue pricked deep because it was certain that some of the defendants would be sentenced to death. It seemed that when people had never seen a man, or had seen him only once or twice, they did not find anything offensive about the idea of photographing him while he is being sentenced to death, but that if people had seen him often the idea became unattractive. The correspondents who had attended the court day in day out knew how the defendants had hated the periods of each session when it was part of the routine for the cameras to be put on. Most of them reached for their black glasses when the sharp and acid lights were switched on, with a sullenness which meant that they were doing more than merely trying to save their eyes; and those who most often resorted to those black glasses were those who had manifested the greatest repentance. Dr. Frank, who had murdered Poland and had been driven by remorse into a Catholic conversion which the authorities believed to be sincere, was always the first to put out his hand to his spectacle-case. It might be right to hang these men. But it could not be right to photograph them when they were being told that they were going to be hanged. For when society has to hurt a man it must hurt him as little as possible and must preserve what it can of his pride, lest there should spread in that society those feelings which make men do the things for which they get hanged.

But though it might be right to hang these men, it was not easy. A sadness fell on the lawyers engaged in the trial. They had all been waiting for this day when judgment would be delivered and the defendants sentenced. They had all surely come to loathe the Nazi crimes and criminals more and more in the slow unfolding of the case. But now this day of judgment had come, they were not happy. There

from **"Greenhouse with Cyclamens—I"** by Rebecca West

←—Response notes—→

was a gloom about the places where they lived, a gloom about their families. In these last days of the trial all automobiles were stopped on the main roads for search and scrutiny by the military police. At a search-post two automobiles were halted at the same time, and a visitor travelling in one saw that in the other was the wife of one of the judges, a tall Scandinavian notable for her physical and spiritual graces. They exchanged greetings and the visitor said, "I shall be seeing you in court tomorrow." The other looked as if she had been slapped across the high cheekbones. "Oh, no," she said, "Oh, no. I shall not be in court tomorrow." Yet she had attended almost all previous sessions of the court. Around the house of another English judge a line of cars waited all the evening before the verdicts day and passers-by knew that the judiciary was holding its last conference. The judge's wife came to the window and looked out over the automobiles and the passers-by into the pinewoods which ringed the house. But as she stared out into the darkening woods it could be seen on her sensitive face that she was living through a desert of time comparable to the interval between a death and a funeral.

There was another house in the outskirts of Nuremberg where this profound aversion from the consequences of the trial could be perceived. This, like the Press Camp, was a villa which an industrialist had built beside his factory, but it was smaller and not so gross, and it had been the scene of a war of taste which had in the long run been won by the right side. The industrialist had furnished it like a Nord Deutscher Lloyd liner; but he had had two sons, who, according to the patriarchal system of his class, lived in the villa, the older on the first floor, the younger on the top floor. One of them had married a Frenchwoman who was still in the house, silently and efficiently acting as butler to the conquerors, with an exquisite and chivalrous care not to detach herself from the conquered, since her marriage vows had placed her in their company. She had a deep knowledge and love of Greek art, and of the minor Italian masters of the sixteenth and seventeenth centuries. Most of her collections had been taken from her at the beginning of the war by the German government and stored in caves. When defeat came the guards in charge of the caves ran away, and the stores were rifled. She had gone there to look for her goods, and had found some shards of her Greek vases trodden into the earth at the mouth of the caves, and nothing else. But she had insisted on keeping with her some of her Greek sculptures, and they still stood in the house among monstrous Japanese bronzes and moustachioed busts of the men of the family. In one room there were two marbles which, in the Greek way, presented the whole truth about certain moments of physical existence. There was a torso which showed how it is with a boy's body, cut clean with training, when the ribs rise to a deep and enjoyed breath; and there was the coiffed head of a girl who knew she was being looked at by the world, and being proud and innocent, let it look.

The approach to this house at night was melancholy. About it, as about all houses inhabited by legal personnel, armed guards paced, and

from **"Greenhouse with Cyclamens—I"** by Rebecca West

searchlights shone into the woods. The white beams changed to crudely coloured cardboard the piebald trunks of the birch trees, the small twisted pines, the great pottery jars overflowing with nasturtiums which marked the course of the avenues. From the darkness above, moth-pale birch leaves fell slowly, turned suddenly bright yellow in the searchlight beam, and drifted slowly down to the illuminated ground. Autumn was here, winter would be here soon. People concerned with the trial drove through these sad avenues and were welcomed into the house, and sat about in its great rooms, holding glasses of good wine in their hands, and talked generously of pleasant things and not of the judgment and the sentences, and looked at the Greek sculptures with a certain wonder and awe and confusion. If a trial for murder lasts too long, more than the murder will out. The man in the murderer will out; it becomes horrible to think of destroying him.

●◆ How does West feel about capital punishment? Return to the text and underline the direct statements that reveal her attitude. Briefly summarize her reasons.

....

....

....

....

●◆ Rebecca West structures her report by moving from minor episodes to broader thinking on the subject. Select one episode or concrete image, such as seeing the judge's Scandinavian wife or the Greek statues. Explain how it relates to her thoughts about human nature and capital punishment.

....

....

....

....

....

....

....

Noticing
the minor episodes and concrete images that writers use can help you interpret their broader meaning.

Four Reading an Argumentative Essay

Understanding the structure a writer uses is an important part of interpreting an argument. For example, a cause-and-effect structure reinforces the writer's ideas about how events or phenomena are interrelated. A compare-and-contrast structure shows how phenomena conflict.

In *An Experiment in Criticism*, C. S. Lewis proposed a radical change in how we judge books. Rather than focusing on the quality of the book, he suggests that we focus on the characteristics of the reader. As you read an excerpt from his book, notice how Lewis constructs his argument.

from *An Experiment in Criticism* by C. S. Lewis

← Response notes →

In this essay I propose to try an experiment. Literary criticism is traditionally employed in judging books. Any judgement it implies about men's reading of books is a corollary from its judgement on the books themselves. Bad taste is, as it were by definition, a taste for bad books. I want to find out what sort of picture we shall get by reversing the process. Let us make our distinction between readers or types of reading the basis, and our distinction between books the corollary. Let us try to discover how far it might be plausible to define a good book as a book which is read in one way, and a bad book as a book which is read in another.

I think this worth trying because the normal procedure seems to me to involve almost continually a false implication. If we say that *A* likes (or has a taste for) the women's magazines and *B* likes (or has a taste for) Dante, this sounds as if *likes* and *taste* have the same meaning when applied to both; as if there were a single activity, though the objects to which it is directed are different. But observation convinces me that this, at least usually, is untrue.

Already in our schooldays some of us were making our first responses to good literature. Others, and these the majority, were reading, at school, *The Captain,* and, at home, short-lived novels from the circulating library. But it was apparent then that the majority did not "like" their fare in the way we "liked" ours. It is apparent still. The differences leap to the eye.

In the first place, the majority never read anything twice. The sure mark of an unliterary man is that he considers "I've read it already" to be a conclusive argument against reading a work. We have all known women who remembered a novel so dimly that they had to stand for half an hour in the library skimming through it before they were certain they had once read it. But the moment they became certain, they rejected it immediately. It was for them dead, like a burnt-out match, an old railway ticket or yesterday's paper; they had already used it. Those who read great works, on the other hand, will read the same work ten, twenty or thirty times during the course of their life.

Secondly, the majority, though they are sometimes frequent readers, do not set much store by reading. They turn to it as a last resource. They abandon it with alacrity as soon as any alternative pastime turns up. It is kept for railway journeys, illnesses, odd

from *An Experiment in Criticism* by C. S. Lewis

←—Response notes—→

moments of enforced solitude, or for the process called "reading oneself to sleep." They sometimes combine it with desultory conversation; often, with listening to the radio. But literary people are always looking for leisure and silence in which to read and do so with their whole attention. When they are denied such attentive and undisturbed reading even for a few days they feel impoverished.

Thirdly, the first reading of some literary work is often, to the literary, an experience so momentous that only experiences of love, religion, or bereavement can furnish a standard of comparison. Their whole consciousness is changed. They have become what they were not before. But there is no sign of anything like this among the other sort of readers. When they have finished the story or the novel, nothing much, or nothing at all, seems to have happened to them.

Finally, and as a natural result of their different behaviour in reading, what they have read is constantly and prominently present to the mind of the few, but not to that of the many. The former mouth over their favourite lines and stanzas in solitude. Scenes and characters from books provide them with a sort of iconography by which they interpret or sum up their own experience. They talk to one another about books, often and at length. The latter seldom think or talk of their reading.

It is pretty clear that the majority, if they spoke without passion and were fully articulate, would not accuse us of liking the wrong books, but of making such a fuss about any books at all. We treat as a main ingredient in our well-being something which to them is marginal. Hence to say simply that they like one thing and we another is to leave out nearly the whole of the facts. If *like* is the correct word for what they do to books, some other word must be found for what we do. Or, conversely, if we *like* our kind of book we must not say that they *like* any book. If the few have "good taste," then we may have to say that no such thing as "bad taste" exists: for the inclination which the many have to their sort of reading is not the same thing and, if the word were univocally used, would not be called taste at all.

Though I shall concern myself almost entirely with literature, it is worth noting that the same difference of attitude is displayed about the other arts and about natural beauty. Many people enjoy popular music in a way which is compatible with humming the tune, stamping in time, talking, and eating. And when the popular tune has once gone out of fashion they enjoy it no more. Those who enjoy Bach react quite differently. Some buy pictures because the walls "look so bare without them"; and after the pictures have been in the house for a week they become practically invisible to them. But there are a few who feed on a great picture for years. As regards nature, the majority "like a nice view as well as anyone." They are not saying a word against it. But to make the landscapes a really important factor in, say, choosing the place for a holiday—to put them on a level with such serious considerations as a luxurious hotel, a good golf links, and a sunny climate—would seem to them affectation. To "go on" about them like Wordsworth would be humbug.

●◆ One task in analyzing the structure of an argumentative essay is to find the thesis statement. Lewis explicitly states his purpose in the beginning of the excerpt. Underline that statement. Then, summarize the key points of Lewis' argument.

....

....

....

....

●◆ Do you agree with Lewis? Some readers have thought that he was elitist. Others have observed the same behaviors he notes. Write an argument that either defends or argues against his main point. Use your own observations or experiences to support it.

....

....

....

....

....

....

....

....

....

....

....

....

....

....

....

....

Understanding
the structure of an
argumentative essay helps
you identify and respond
to key points.

Five

Understanding Arguments

Writers need to consider possible objections as they develop their arguments. C. S. Lewis was aware that his definitions of "the many" and "the few" needed more development than he gave them in the first chapter of *An Experiment in Criticism*. In the next chapter, he refined his definitions. He noted that the barriers between the two groups were not fixed and that many people moved from one group to another throughout their lifetimes. Read the conclusion of Chapter Two.

from *An Experiment in Criticism* by C. S. Lewis

← *Response notes* →

Can we then, since all else fails, characterize the literary "few" as *mature* readers? There will certainly be this much truth in the adjective; that excellence in our response to books, like excellence in other things, cannot be had without experience and discipline, and therefore cannot be had by the very young. But some of the truth still escapes us. If we are suggesting that all men naturally begin by treating literature like the many, and that all who, in their general psychology, succeed in becoming mature will also learn to read like the few, I believe we are wrong. I think the two kinds of readers are already foreshadowed in the nursery. Before they can read at all, while literature comes before them as stories not read but listened to, do not children react to it differently? Certainly, as soon as they can read for themselves, the two groups are already divided. There are those who read only when there is nothing better to do, gobble up each story to "find out what happened," and seldom go back to it; others who reread and are profoundly moved.

All these attempts to characterize the two sorts of reader are, as I have said, hasty. I have mentioned them to get them out of the way. We must attempt to enter for ourselves into the attitudes involved. This ought to be possible for most of us because most of us, with respect to some of the arts, have passed from one to the other. We know something about the experience of the many not only from observation but from within.

●◆ Throughout the book, Lewis continues to refine his definitions of "the many" and "the few," suggesting that we have probably been part of both groups in our lives. How would you describe yourself as a reader? Are you one of "the many," one of "the few," or one of some group that he has failed to mention?

●◆ Reread the two excerpts from *An Experiment in Criticism* and mark in the text the characteristics of each kind of reader. Write a description of yourself as a reader, using Lewis's characteristics or your own.

Trying to think like the author can help you understand his or her arguments.

Character in Poetry

When we think of characters in literature, we tend to think of fiction rather than poetry. Poems more frequently deal with incidents developed through sensory impressions, reflections, or the exploration of ideas. However, a fair number of them develop rich, full portraits of real or imagined people. The *ode*, for example, is often addressed to a person. The *elegy* is a form of poetry which is used to eulogize or memorialize a real person. Less formal types of poems are often memoirs or rememberances of people important in the writer's life.

Character in poetry is often revealed in subtle ways. In narrative poems, writers may show a character in action. The picture of the character builds as the story unfolds. In lyric poems, writers are more likely to use metaphors and symbols. They often use allusions, comparing a character to people in history or myth. In these poems, readers must do more work, sometimes even looking up references they do not know. The richer your own knowledge and the more extensive your reading has been, the easier it is for you to enjoy poetic portraits.

Read George Barker's sonnet "To My Mother." Use the response notes to write your questions, comments about the meaning, or other thoughts that occur to you as you read. François Rabelais, mentioned in line five, was a sixteenth-century French writer famed as a satirist.

Response notes

To My Mother
George Barker

Most near, most dear, most loved and most far,
Under the window where I often found her
Sitting as huge as Asia, seismic with laughter,
Gin and chicken helpless in her Irish hand,
Irresistible as Rabelais but most tender for
The lame dogs and hurt birds that surround her,—
She is a procession no one can follow after
But be like a little dog following a brass band.

She will not glance up at the bomber or condescend
To drop her gin and scuttle to a cellar,
But lean on the mahogany table like a mountain
Whom only faith can move, and so I send
O all my faith, and all my love to tell her
That she will move from mourning into morning.

Reread "To My Mother" looking specifically at how George Barker uses various **figures of speech** to develop the character of his mother. Underline and identify in the response notes examples of **similes**, **metaphors**, and **allusions**.

Discuss the following questions with a partner. Write down your final ideas about these questions.

●◆ How do the figures of speech help you build up a picture of the woman?

....

●◆ How do the last lines of the poem and the first line relate to each other?

....

●◆ What similes or metaphors would you use to describe the mother? For example, what kind of animal is she most like? What kind of plant? Write four or five comparisons.

Writers use metaphors and allusions as a way to create a well-defined portrait.

....

....

....

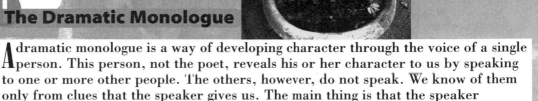

Two

The Dramatic Monologue

A dramatic monologue is a way of developing character through the voice of a single person. This person, not the poet, reveals his or her character to us by speaking to one or more other people. The others, however, do not speak. We know of them only from clues that the speaker gives us. The main thing is that the speaker unintentionally reveals his own character as he talks.

In Robert Browning's "My Last Duchess," probably the most famous **dramatic monologue** ever written, a duke negotiates with an ambassador for the hand of the count's daughter in marriage.

My Last Duchess
Robert Browning

Response notes

Ferrara

That's my last Duchess painted on the wall,
Looking as if she were alive. I call
That piece a wonder, now: Frà Pandolf's hands
Worked busily a day, and there she stands.
Will't please you sit and look at her? I said
"Frà Pandolf" by design, for never read
Strangers like you that pictured countenance,
The depth and passion of its earnest glance,
But to myself they turned (since none puts by
The curtain I have drawn for you, but I)
And seemed as they would ask me, if they durst,
How such a glance came there; so, not the first
Are you to turn and ask thus. Sir, 'twas not
Her husband's presence only, called that spot
Of joy into the Duchess' cheek; perhaps
Frà Pandolf chanced to say, "Her mantle laps
Over my lady's wrist too much," or "Paint
Must never hope to reproduce the faint
Half-flush that dies along her throat": such stuff
Was courtesy, she thought, and cause enough
For calling up that spot of joy. She had
A heart—how shall I say?—too soon made glad,
Too easily impressed: she liked whate'er
She looked on, and her looks went everywhere.
Sir, 'twas all one! My favour at her breast,
The dropping of the daylight in the West,
The bough of cherries some officious fool
Broke in the orchard for her, the white mule
She rode with round the terrace—all and each
Would draw from her alike the approving speech.
Or blush, at least. She thanked men,—good! But thanked
Somehow—I know not how—as if she ranked
My gift of a nine-hundred-years-old name
With anybody's gift. Who'd stoop to blame
This sort of trifling? Even had you skill
In speech— (which I have not)—to make your will

179

Response notes

MY LAST DUCHESS (continued)

Quite clear to such an one, and say, "Just this
Or that in you disgusts me; here you miss,
Or there exceed the mark" —and if she let
Herself be lessoned so, nor plainly set
Her wits to yours, forsooth, and made excuse,
—E'en then would be some stooping; and I choose
Never to stoop. Oh sir, she smiled, not doubt,
Whene'er I passed her; but who passed without
Much the same smile? This grew; I gave commands;
Then all smiles stopped together. There she stands
As if alive. Will't please you rise? We'll meet
The company below, then. I repeat,
The Count your master's known munificence
Is ample warrant that no just pretense
Of mine for dowry will be disallowed;
Though his fair daughter's self, as I avowed
At starting, is my object. Nay, we'll go
Together down, sir. Notice Neptune, though,
Taming a sea-horse, thought a rarity,
Which Claus of Innsbruck cast in bronze for me!

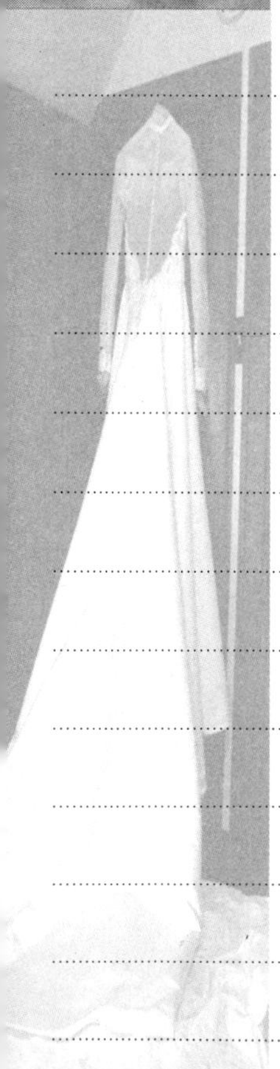

180

Why is the duke negotiating for a new wife? What do you think happened to his "last duchess"? Why?

In column one of the chart below, record words, phrases, or lines that describe the duke. In column two, explain what these quotations say about his character.

Words, phrases, lines that describe the duke	What these quotations say about his character

➥ Write a brief character sketch of the duke as if you were describing him to someone who had not read the poem.

A dramatic monologue is structured to focus your attention on the character of the speaker as he or she unintentionally reveals it in the course of the poem.

William Butler Yeats was one of the most important poets of the twentieth century. In the elegy "In Memory of W. B. Yeats," we learn what another important poet, W. H. Auden, thought about the man, the artist, and his art. The poem is in three parts. In this lesson you will read the first part.

Response notes

In Memory of W. B. Yeats (d. January 1939)
W. H. Auden

1

He disappeared in the dead of winter:
The brooks were frozen, the air-ports almost deserted,
And snow disfigured the public statues;
The mercury sank in the mouth of the dying day.
O all the instruments agree
The day of his death was a dark cold day.

Far from his illness
The wolves ran on through the evergreen forests,
The peasant river was untempted by the fashionable quays;
By mourning tongues
The death of the poet was kept from his poems.

But for him it was his last afternoon as himself,
An afternoon of nurses and rumours;
The provinces of his body revolted,
The squares of his mind were empty,
Silence invaded the suburbs,
The current of his feeling failed: he became his admirers.

Now he is scattered among a hundred cities
And wholly given over to unfamiliar affections;
To find his happiness in another kind of wood
And be punished under a foreign code of conscience.
The words of a dead man
Are modified in the guts of the living.

But in the importance and noise of to-morrow
When the brokers are roaring like beasts on the floor of the Bourse,
And the poor have the sufferings to which they are fairly accustomed,
And each in the cell of himself is almost convinced of his freedom;
A few thousand will think of this day
As one thinks of a day when one did something slightly unusual.

O all the instruments agree
The day of his death was a dark cold day.

Formulate three or four questions about this part of the poem. They may be questions about the language, specific lines or phrases, or about Yeats himself. After you have written your questions, write some possible answers to them. If you can't think of any possibilities, jot down what resources you might use to find some answers.

Questions	Possible Answers
Example: What does "The wolves ran on through the evergreen forests" mean?	I think that Auden means that the wolves and the forests are simpy there. They have nothing to do with poetry. They remain the same even though the world has lost this great man.

The first line of the poem—"He disappeared in the dead of winter"—sets the tone and creates the dominant metaphor for this section of the poem, the seasonal landscape. Make a list of the various landscapes depicted in the first part of the poem. Then write a description of how you think they relate to the death of the poet.

List of Landscapes	Relation to the Death of the Poet

Asking yourself questions and attempting to answer them is a useful strategy in dealing with complex pieces of literature. Work through the possible answers to your questions until you feel confident in your understanding.

In the second part of "In Memory of W. B. Yeats," Auden changes **tone** and **style**. Jot down questions and ideas as you read.

Response notes

In Memory of W. B. Yeats (d. January 1939)
W. H. Auden

2

You were silly like us: your gift survived it all;
The parish of rich women, physical decay,
Yourself; mad Ireland hurt you into poetry.
Now Ireland has her madness and her weather still,
For poetry makes nothing happen: it survives
In the valley of its saying where executives
Would never want to tamper; it flows south
From ranches of isolation and the busy griefs,
Raw towns that we believe and die in; it survives,
A way of happening, a mouth.

The appearance of the *you* in the poem marks a change. Yeats, who in the first part was a distant third person, is suddenly present as the person being addressed. In this case, we quickly see that Auden is addressing Yeats, but because of the **you**, we are invited into the position of reading as if we were Yeats.

●◆ Summarize what you think Auden is saying about Yeats in this section.

●◆ What do you think the phrase "poetry makes nothing happen" means in the context of the poem?

The use of the second person draws us into the poem and makes us read both as ourselves and as the subject being addressed in the poem.

Five
Completing the Reading

In the last section, Auden again changes the **tone** and **style**. He begins by addressing the Earth, which is about to receive the body of the dead poet. Later, he again addresses Yeats. Read this section slowly, as if you could hear marching feet and perhaps the occasional sound of a distant cannon.

In Memory of W. B. Yeats (d. January 1939)
W. H. Auden

3

Earth, receive an honoured guest;
William Yeats is laid to rest:
Let the Irish vessel lie
Emptied of its poetry.

In the nightmare of the dark
All the dogs of Europe bark,
And the living nations wait,
Each sequestered in its hate;

Intellectual disgrace
Stares from every human face,
And the seas of pity lie
Locked and frozen in each eye.

Follow, poet, follow right
To the bottom of the night,
With your unconstraining Voice
Still persuade us to rejoice;

With the farming of a verse
Make a vineyard of the curse,
Sing of human unsuccess
In a rapture of distress;

In the deserts of the heart
Let the healing fountain start,
In the prison of his days
Teach the free man how to praise.

●◆ What do you think Auden is saying about time and language?

It is time now to put the poem back together. Read all three sections, one after the other, as they are intended to be read. It is best if you read it aloud or listen to it read aloud. That way you can clearly hear the changes of tone.

Compare the ending of the poem to the opening. Notice that it moves from images of winter landscapes on the day of Yeats' death to a "vineyard" and a "healing fountain." Notice, too, that although some of the references in the poem are obscure, Auden is writing about more than Yeats as a person. He is also writing about what poetry is and its place in society.

●◆ Write your ideas about what Auden is saying about Yeats, about poetry, and about art in general.

The long poem generally focuses on a subject from a variety of angles, leading the reader toward an idea or theme through all the sections of the poem.

Poetry and Art

Poets paint with words. They describe the ugly and the beautiful, the sorrows of life and the joys. Many poems focus on the impermanence of life, which is, ironically, what the poet is trying to stave off through art. T. S. Eliot expressed that quality of timelessness as the "still point of the turning world." "Except for the point, the still point," he wrote, "there would be no dance, and there is only the dance."

Eliot has no question about the importance of poetry in the world. Poets, like all artists, reflect and distill the ideas that concern us. Painters do it with color and image, composers with notes and melody, poets with words.

One The Art of Irony

Percy Bysshe Shelley was a brilliant poet who died at the age of thirty. He wrote many startling poems during his short lifetime. Read his sonnet "Ozymandias," noting your questions and comments as you read.

Response notes

Ozymandias
Percy Bysshe Shelley

I met a traveler from an antique land
Who said: Two vast and trunkless legs of stone
Stand in the desert. Near them, on the sand,
Half sunk, a shattered visage lies, whose frown,
And wrinkled lip, and sneer of cold command,
Tell that its sculptor well those passions read
Which yet survive, stamped on these lifeless things,
The hand that mocked them and the heart that fed;
And on the pedestal these words appear:
"My name is Ozymandias, king of kings:
Look on my works, ye Mighty, and despair!"
Nothing beside remains. Round the decay
Of that colossal wreck, boundless and bare
The lone and level sands stretch far away.

188

●◆ What are your first thoughts about the meaning of this poem?

Lines four to eight of the poem are rather tricky grammatically. Study the passage and answer the following four questions:

●◆ Whose passions? What passions? Whose hand? Whose heart?

The poem displays what is known as **situational irony**. This form of **figurative language** involves some kind of apparent contradiction between what is real and what is imagined, or between what one anticipates and what actually happens.

●◆ What is the discrepancy between the words on the pedestal and the current state of the statue?

....

....

....

Go back now and reread the whole poem, looking for words, phrases, or sentences that have to do with power, time, or art. Mark those passages and jot down comments in your response notes about the meaning of the lines you select.

●◆ Write your ideas about how Shelley uses the irony of the situation to make comments about power, time, and art.

....

....

....

189

....

....

....

....

....

....

....

....

....

....

....

....

Writers use irony to point out the differences between what is imagined and what is.

John Keats, a contemporary of Shelley, lived an even shorter life. He wrote so many poems that it is hard to imagine that he died of tuberculosis when he was only twenty-six. Keats was writing in the early-nineteenth century and used such words as *canst*, *thou*, and *ye*. Good readers learn to work through any differences in language.

An **ode** is a poem addressing someone or something directly. In this poem, Keats begins by addressing a Grecian urn or vase. Since this is a fairly long poem, you will read the first part of it in this lesson. In the next lesson, you will read the rest of the poem.

Response notes

Ode on a Grecian Urn
John Keats

Thou still unravished bride of quietness,
   Thou foster-child of silence and slow time,
Sylvan historian, who canst thus express
   A flowery tale more sweetly than our rhyme:
What leaf-fringed legend haunts about thy shape
   Of deities or mortals, or of both,
      In Tempe or the dales of Arcady?
   What men or gods are these? What maidens loth?
What mad pursuit? What struggle to escape?
   What pipes and timbrels? What wild ecstasy?

Heard melodies are sweet, but those unheard
   Are sweeter; therefore, ye soft pipes, play on;
Not to the sensual ear, but, more endeared,
   Pipe to the spirit ditties of no tone:
Fair youth, beneath the trees, thou canst not leave
   Thy song, nor ever can those trees be bare;
      Bold Lover, never, never canst thou kiss,
Though winning near the goal—yet, do not grieve;
      She cannot fade, though thou has not thy bliss,
   For ever wilt thou love, and she be fair!

Ah, happy, happy boughs! that cannot shed
   Your leaves, nor ever bid the Spring adieu;
And, happy melodist, unwearied,
   For ever piping songs for ever new;
More happy love! more happy, happy love!
   For ever warm and still to be enjoyed,
      For ever panting, and for ever young;
All breathing human passion far above,
   That leaves a heart high-sorrowful and cloyed,
      A burning forehead, and a parching tongue.

In the outline of a Greek vase below, draw part of the scene that Keats describes. Around the vase, write the lines from the poem that you have chosen to draw in your picture.

191

●◆Make notes about Keats' idea that in art all things are forever possible. In "Ode on a Grecian Urn," for example, trees never shed their leaves, the music is always perfect, the lovers never grow old and never fall out of love. Make up your own scene that expresses Keats' ideas.

Visualizing
a scene depicted by a writer is an important step toward understanding the meaning.

Now read the second part of "Ode on a Grecian Urn" and use the response notes to sketch the scene that is portrayed on this side of the urn. Continue to jot down ideas about the meaning of the poem.

Response notes

Ode on a Grecian Urn (continued)
John Keats

Who are these coming to the sacrifice?
    To what green altar, O mysterious priest,
Lead'st thou that heifer lowing at the skies,
    And all her silken flanks with garlands drest?
What little town by river or sea shore,
    Or mountain-built with peaceful citadel,
        Is emptied of this folk, this pious morn?
And, little town, thy streets for evermore
    Will silent be; and not a soul to tell
        Why thou art desolate, can e'er return.

O Attic shape! Fair attitude! With brede
    Of marble men and maidens overwrought,
With forest branches and the trodden weed;
    Thou, silent form, dost tease us out of thought
As doth Eternity: Cold Pastoral!
    When old age shall this generation waste,
        Thou shalt remain, in midst of other woe
    Than ours, a friend to man, to whom thou say'st,
Beauty is truth, truth beauty,—that is all
    Ye know on earth, and all ye need to know.

●◆ What scene is pictured in the first ten lines of this side of the urn?

....

....

●◆ In the last stanza of this poem the narrator addresses the urn directly. What you think Keats means when he says, "Beauty is truth, truth beauty"?

....

....

●◆ What does the narrator mean by this last statement: "that is all / Ye know on earth, and all ye need to know"? What do you think about this idea?

....

....

●✧Reread the entire poem. Then describe what you think Keats is saying about time, art, beauty, and truth. Include quotations and direct references to the poem as you explain your ideas.

Poetry is often ambiguous. It is important to keep all the possibilities of interpretation open as you read and think about a poem.

Here is another poem that takes up the question
Keats was exploring in "Ode on a Grecian Urn."

A Rhinoceros and a Lion
Kaoru Maruyama

A rhinoceros was running;
  A lion was clinging to his back,
  Biting.

Blood spouted up and, twisting his neck in agony,
The rhinoceros was looking at the sky.
The sky was blue and quiet.
The daytime moon floated in it.

It was a picture,
An accidental moment in a far country of jungles,
So the landscape was silent,
The two animals remained as they were.
Only in the stillness
The lion was, moment by moment, trying to kill;
The rhinoceros was, eternally, about to die.

194

●◆ Sketch the scene in the painting that Maruyama is describing.

Share your sketch with a partner or group. Compare your reading of the poem
as indicated by what you chose to include or not include. Discuss the lines that you
used to make your sketch.

●◆ What do "A Rhinoceros and a Lion" and "Ode on a Grecian Urn" have in common? What does Keats do that Maruyama docs not do? How do you think Maruyama's poem is similar to and different from Keats's poem?

195

Comparing poems on the same theme is a way of gaining new perspectives on them.

T. S. Eliot is well known for the lighthearted poems in *Old Possum's Book of Practical Cats*, which were the basis for the musical *Cats*. However, most of his poems are complex inquiries into philosophical questions. His *Four Quartets* are related poems examining the nature of time and art.

As you read an excerpt from *Four Quartets*, make quick sketches that respond to the words of the poem with whatever images or thoughts come to you.

Response notes

from "Burnt Norton" from *Four Quartets*
T. S. Eliot

Words move, music moves
Only in time; but that which is only living
Can only die. Words, after speech, reach
Into the silence. Only by the form, the pattern,
Can words or music reach
The stillness, as a Chinese jar still
Moves perpetually in its stillness.
Not the stillness of the violin, while the note lasts,
Not that only, but the co-existence,
Or say that the end precedes the beginning,
And the end and the beginning were always there
Before the beginning and after the end.
And all is always now. Words strain,
Crack and sometimes break, under the burden,
Under the tension, slip, slide, perish,
Decay with imprecision, will not stay in place,
Will not stay still. Shrieking voices
Scolding, mocking, or merely chattering,
Always assail them. The Word in the desert
Is most attacked by voices of temptation,
The crying shadow in the funeral dance,
The loud lament of the disconsolate chimera.

The detail of the pattern is movement,
As in the figure of the ten stairs.
Desire itself is movement
Not in itself desirable;
Love is itself unmoving,
Only the cause and end of movement,
Timeless, and undesiring
Except in the aspect of time
Caught in the form of limitation
Between un-being and being.
Sudden in a shaft of sunlight
Even while the dust moves
There rises the hidden laughter
Of children in the foliage
Quick now, here, now, always—
Ridiculous the waste sad time
Stretching before and after.

●◆ Write your interpretation of what each of the following quotations means in the context of the theme "poetry and art."

. . . Only by the form, the pattern,
Can words or music reach
The stillness, as a Chinese jar still
Moves perpetually in its stillness.

197

Words, after speech, reach
Into the silence

Love is itself unmoving,
Only the cause and end of movement

●◆Now reread the poem. Underline any word or words that stand out for you; anything from a simple word or a short phrase to an entire sentence. Be sure you underline at least 12 to 15 words or phrases. When you have finished, use the words that you have underlined to put together a poem of your own. Title your poem with a word or phrase from Eliot's poem. (This strategy of composing a poem is called "found poetry.")

●◆ What did you learn about Eliot's poem from your annotations and your found poem?

An interpretation of a poem needs to be based on both analysis and reflection. Exploring the language and ideas of a poem will help you solidify your ideas and construct your interpretation.

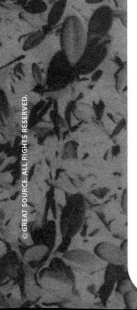

Focus on the Writer: V. S. Naipaul

V. S. Naipaul is one of the most highly regarded writers in the world. He has received numerous awards and is often mentioned as a future winner of the Nobel Prize in Literature. The critic Irving Howe wrote, "For sheer abundance of talent there can hardly be a writer alive who surpasses V. S. Naipaul."

Naipaul was born in 1932 on the Caribbean island of Trinidad, a colony of Britain. Growing up on a dependent island that later struggled to cope with independence left a deep impression on Naipaul. Moreover, his family was from India, seperating them from the native West Indians. One of his major themes is rootlessness. His search to find a home and a tradition where he can belong has taken him from Trinidad to India and to England. Naipaul finally identifies himself as a man of the world rather than of one culture.

Naipaul is a prolific writer who has published more than twenty works of fiction and nonfiction. His novels and his travel books are equally important in explaining his viewpoints and ideas. His first novel was published when he was twenty-three, and he is proud to say that he has had no profession in his lifetime other than writer.

One Creating Characters

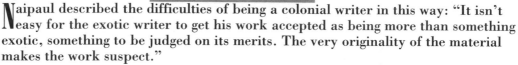

Naipaul described the difficulties of being a colonial writer in this way: "It isn't easy for the exotic writer to get his work accepted as being more than something exotic, something to be judged on its merits. The very originality of the material makes the work suspect."

The first book Naipaul wrote was a collection of sketches based on people he had known in Trinidad. Although it was not published until he had established his reputation as a novelist, *Miguel Street* shows the young author's ability to create characters.

← Response notes →

from "Hat" from *Miguel Street* by V. S. Naipaul

I never knew a man who enjoyed life as much as Hat did. He did nothing new or spectacular—in fact, he did practically the same things every day—but he always enjoyed what he did. And every now and then he managed to give a fantastic twist to some very ordinary thing.

He was a bit like his dog. This was the tamest Alsatian I have ever known. One of the things I noticed in Miguel Street was the way dogs resembled their owners. George had a surly, mean mongrel. Toni's dog was a terrible savage. Hat's dog was the only Alsatian I knew with a sense of humour.

In the first place it behaved oddly, for an Alsatian. You could make it the happiest dog on earth if you flung things for it to retrieve. One day, in the Savannah, I flung a guava into some thick bushes. He couldn't get at the guava, and he whined and complained. He suddenly turned and ran back past me, barking loudly. While I turned to see what was wrong, he ran back to the bushes. I saw nothing strange, and when I looked back I was just in time to see him taking another guava behind the bushes.

I called him and he rushed up whining and barking.

I said, "Go on, boy. Go on and get the guava."

He ran back to the bushes and poked and sniffed a bit and then dashed behind the bushes to get the guava he had himself placed there.

I only wish the beautiful birds Hat collected were as tame as the Alsatian. The macaws and the parrots looked like angry and quarrelsome old women and they attacked anybody. Sometimes Hat's house became a dangerous place with all these birds around. You would be talking quietly when you would suddenly feel a prick and a tug on your calf. The macaw or the parrot. Hat tried to make us believe they didn't bite him, but I know that they did.

In this excerpt, Naipaul uses an indirect method to characterize Hat; he lets the reader infer qualities by describing the man's pets. What guesses can you make about Hat based on this description?

➤➤ Try this method of characterization for yourself. Imagine a person that you could characterize indirectly, using some possessions or habits. Describe them clearly enough that the reader can infer key aspects of your character's personality.

To create believable characters, writers use details and descriptions to answer the question, "What makes this character distinct?"

Two Replaying the Newsreel

Naipaul is a careful observer with an excellent memory. These abilities are essential to him as he recreates the society and characters around him in his books. In a conversation with Mel Gussow of *The New York Times*, Naipaul explained he would record every meaningful experience in his memory by playing "the newsreel back." "I'll not only replay the words . . . I'll replay the face—constantly, everything." Then as he writes, he carefully reshapes his observations to create the overall effect he wants to achieve.

In 1994, Naipaul published an autobiographical novel about a writer trying to understand himself. Below is an excerpt from *A Way in the World*: *A Novel*.

"Prelude: An Inheritance" from ***A Way in the World: A Novel***
by V. S. Naipaul

← Response notes →

I left home more than forty years ago. I was eighteen. When I went back, after six years—and slowly: a two-week journey by steamer—everything was strange and not strange: the suddenness of night, the very big leaves of some trees, the shrunken streets, the corrugated-iron roofs. You could walk down a street and hear the American advertising jingles coming out of the Rediffusion sets in all the little open houses. Six years before I had known the jingles the Rediffusion sets played; but these jingles were all new to me and were like somebody else's folksong now.

All the people on the streets were darker than I remembered: Africans, Indians, whites, Portuguese, mixed Chinese. In their houses, though, people didn't look so dark. I suppose that was because on the streets I was more of a looker, half a tourist, and when I went to a house it was to be with people I had known years before. So I saw them more easily.

To go back home was to play with impressions in this way, the way I played with the first pair of glasses I had, looking at a world now sharp and small and not quite real, now standard size and real but blurred; the way I played with my first pair of dark glasses, moving between dazzle and coolness; or the way, on this first return, when I was introduced to air-conditioning, I liked to move from the coolness of an air-conditioned room to the warmth outside, and back again. I was in time, over the years, and over many returns, to get used to what was new; but that shifting about of reality never really stopped. I could call it up whenever I wished. Up to about twenty years ago whenever I went back I could persuade myself from time to time that I was in a half-dream, knowing and not knowing. It was a pleasant feeling; it was a little like the sensations that came to me as a child when, once in the rainy season, I had "fever."

Take a few minutes to consider the opening of this story. Knowing that Naipaul left Trinidad to study at Oxford when he was eighteen, we can question how much of the story will be autobiography and how much fiction. Because he has called *A Way in the World* a novel, we cannot assume that the narrator is the author. Closely examine his technique by circling in the text the places where he emphasizes memory. Underline the sections that seem to be imaginary.

202

"Prelude: An Inheritance" from *A Way in the World: A Novel*
by V. S. Naipaul

← *Response notes* →

It was at a time like that, a time of "fever," during a return, that I heard about Leonard Side, a decorator of cakes and arranger of flowers. I heard about him from a school teacher.

The school she taught at was a new one, beyond the suburbs of the town, and in what had been country and plantations right up to the end of the war. The school grounds still looked like a piece of a cleared sugar-cane or coconut estate. There wasn't even a tree. The plain two-storey concrete building—green roof, cream-coloured walls—stood by itself in the openness and the glare.

The teacher said, "The work we were doing in those early days was a little bit like social work, with girls from labouring families. Some of them had brothers or fathers or relations who had gone to jail; they talked about this in the most natural way. One day, at a staff meeting in that very hot school with the glare all around, one of the senior teachers, a Presbyterian Indian lady, suggested that we should have a May Day fair, to introduce the girls to that idea. Everybody agreed, and we decided that the thing to do would be to ask the girls to make flower displays or arrangements, and to give a prize to the girl who did the best display.

"If you had a prize you had to have a judge. If you didn't have a good judge the idea wouldn't work. Who was this judge to be? The people we taught were very cynical. They got it from their families. Oh, they were very respectful and so on, but they thought that everybody and everything was crooked, and in their heart of hearts they looked down on the people above them. So we couldn't have a judge from the government or the Education Department or anybody too famous. This didn't leave us with too many names.

"One of the junior teachers, very young, a country girl herself, fresh from the GTC, the Government Training College, then said that Leonard Side would make the perfect judge.

"Who was Leonard Side?

"The girl had to think. Then she said, 'He work all his life in flowers.'

"Well. But then somebody else remembered the name. She said Leonard Side gave little courses at the WAA, the Women's Auxiliary Association, and people there liked him. That was the place to find him.

"The Women's Auxiliary Association had been founded during the war and was modelled on the WVS in England. They had a building in Parry's Corner, which was in the heart of the city. There was everything in Parry's Corner, a garage for buses, a garage for taxis, a funeral parlour, two cafés, a haberdashery and dry-goods shop, and a number of little houses, some of them offices, some of them dwelling-places; and the well-known Parry family owned it all.

"It was easy for me to go to Parry's Corner, and I offered to go and talk to Leonard Side. The WAA was in a very small building from the Spanish time. The flat front wall—a thick rubble wall, plastered and painted, with rusticated stone slabs at either end—rose up directly from the pavement, so that you stepped from the narrow pavement

←—*Response notes*—→

straight into the front room. The front door was bang in the middle of the pavement wall, and there was a little curtained window on either side. Door and windows had yellow-brown jalousies, linked wooden cross slats you could lift all at once and use an iron pin to close.

"A brown woman was sitting at a desk, and on the dusty wall—dust catching on the unevenness of the plastered rubble wall—were Information Office posters from England. The Tower of London, the English countryside.

"I said, 'They tell me I could find Mr. Side here.'

" 'He over there, across the road,' the woman at the desk said.

"I crossed the road. As always at this time of day, the asphalt was soft and black, as black as the oil-stained concrete floor of the big shed of a garage where the Parry buses were. The building I entered was a modern one, with grey-washed decorated concrete blocks mimicking chipped stone. It was a very clean and plain kind of place, like a doctor's office.

"I said to the girl sitting at the table, 'Mr. Side?'

"She said, 'Go right in.'

"I went through to the inner room, and there I could hardly believe what I saw. A dark Indian man was doing things with his fingers to a dead body on a table or slab in front of him. I had gone to Parry's Funeral Parlour. It was a famous place; it advertised every day on the radio with organ music. I suppose Leonard Side was dressing the body. 'Dressing'—I just knew the word. I had had no idea what it meant. I was too frightened and shocked to say anything. I ran out of the room, and the front room, and got out into the open again. The man ran out after me, calling in a soft voice, 'Miss, Miss.'

"And really he was quite a good-looking man, in spite of the hairy fingers I had seen dressing the dead body on the table. He was very pleased to be asked to judge the girls' flower competition. He even said he wanted to give the first prize. He said that if we allowed him he would make a special posy. And he did, too. A little posy of pink rosebuds. Our May Day fair was a great success.

"A year passed. Fair time came again, and I had to go again and look for Leonard Side. This time I wasn't going to forget: I wasn't going to the funeral parlour. The only place I was going to meet Leonard Side was the Women's Association. I went there late one afternoon after school, about five. The little Spanish-style house was full of women, and in the inside room Leonard Side was doing things with dough, using those hairy fingers to knead dough. Using those fingers to work in a little more milk, then a little more butter.

"He was teaching the women how to make bread and cake. After he had finished doing the dough, he began to teach them how to ice a cake, forcing with those hairy fingers coloured icing out of the special cones or moulds he had. He pressed on and then into the moulds with his hairy fingers, and out came a pink or green rosebud or a flower, which he then fixed with icing-flecked fingers on to the soft iced cake. The women said ooh and aah, and he, very happy with his audience and his work, worked on, like a magician.

"Prelude: An Inheritance" from *A Way in the World: A Novel*
by V. S. Naipaul

"But I didn't like seeing those fingers doing this kind of work, and I liked it less when, at the end, with those same fingers he offered the women little things he had iced, to eat on the spot, as a treat. He liked offering these little treats. They were offered almost like a wafer in church, and the women, concentrating, ate and tasted with a similar kind of respect."

← *Response notes* →

Naipaul juxtaposes impressions and realistic details of the characters and setting to point out various incongruous aspects of the situation.

●◆ Circle five realistic images in the text, such as "icing-flecked fingers." Then list three unusual or odd aspects of the situation or characters on the lines below.

Example: Even though the girls at the school were poor and the school's grounds had no vegetation, the teachers thought the girls should learn how to arrange flowers.

1.

2.

3.

205

Authors do more than report their observations. They often bring out incongruous or unusual details to make their descriptions vivid.

Naipaul knows about being a stranger to oneself. Three cultures have shaped his perspectives: the West Indies, England, and India. He resists being labeled a "West Indian" writer and even cancelled a book contract with a publisher who listed him that way in the catalog. He believes that it is important to cultivate a world perspective rather than a regional one. He says, "One isn't born one's self. One is born with a mass of expectations, a mass of other people's ideas—and you have to work through it all."

In much of his writing, Naipaul highlights the discrepancies between what is suitable in a society and what characters actually do. In the continuation of Leonard Side's story, the teacher is struck—and even offended—by what she views as Mr. Side's inappropriate behavior. Her reaction and Mr. Side's behavior support a common theme in Naipaul's work—the difficulty of finding one's place in the world.

"Prelude: An Inheritance" from *A Way in the World: A Novel*
by V. S. Naipaul

←—Response notes—→

"The third year came. This time I thought I wouldn't go to Parry's Corner to meet Leonard Side. I thought I would go to his house instead. I had found out where he lived. He lived in St. James, quite near where I lived. That was a surprise: that he should have been so close, living that life, and I shouldn't have known.

"I went after school. I was wearing a slender black skirt and a white shirty top and I was carrying a bag with school books. I blew the horn when I stopped. A woman came out to the front gallery, bright in the afternoon light, and she said, 'Come right in.' Just like that, as though she knew me.

"When I went up the steps to the front gallery she said, 'Come in, Doctor. Poor Lenny. He so sick, Doctor.'

"Doctor—that was because of the car and blowing the horn, and the bag, and the clothes I was wearing. I thought I would explain later, and I followed her through this little old St. James wood house to the back room. There I found Leonard Side, very sick and trembling, but dressed for a meeting with the doctor. He was in a shiny brass fourposter bed with a flowered canopy, and he was in green silk pyjamas. His little hairy fingers were resting on the satin or silk spread he was using as a coverlet. He had laid himself out with great care, and the coverlet was folded back neatly.

"There were crepe-paper flowers in a brass vase on a thin-legged side table or vase-stand, and there were satiny cushions and big bows on two simple cane-bottomed bentwood chairs. I knew at once that a lot of that satin and silk had come from the funeral parlour, and was material for the coffins and the laying out of the bodies.

"He was a Mohammedan, everyone knew. But he was so much a man of his job—laying out Christian bodies, though nobody thought of it quite like that—that in that bedroom of his he even had a framed picture of Christ in Majesty, radiating light and gold, and lifting a finger of blessing.

"Prelude: An Inheritance" from *A Way in the World: A Novel*
by V. S. Naipaul

←—Response notes—→

"The picture was centrally placed above the door and leaned forward so much that the blessing of the finger would have seemed aimed at the man on the bed. I knew that the picture wasn't there for the religion alone: it was also for the beauty, the colours, the gold, the long wavy hair of Christ. And I believe I was more shocked than when I saw him dressing the body and later when I saw him using the same fingers to knead dough and then to squeeze out the terrible little blobs of icing.

"It was late afternoon, warm still, and through the open window came the smell of the cesspits of St. James, the cesspits of those dirt yards with the separate little wood houses, two or three to a lot, with runnels of filth from the latrines, runnels that ran green and shiny and then dried away in the dirt; with the discoloured stones where people put out their washing to bleach; with irregular little areas where the earth was mounded up with dust and sand and gravel, and where fruit trees and little shrubs grew, creating the effect not of gardens but of little patches of waste ground where things grew haphazardly.

"When I looked at those hairy fingers on the coverlet and thought about the house and the woman who had called me in—his mother—I wondered about his life and felt sorry and frightened for him. He was sick now; he wanted help. I didn't have the heart to talk to him about the girls and the May Day fair, and I left the house and never saw him again.

"It was his idea of beauty that upset me, I suppose. That idea of beauty had taken him to the job in the funeral parlour, and had got him to deck out his bedroom in the extravagant way he had. That idea of beauty—mixing roses and flowers and nice things to eat with the idea of making the dead human body beautiful too—was contrary to my own idea. The mixing of things upset me. It didn't upset him. I had thought something like that the very first time I had seen him, when he had left his dead body and run out after me to the street, saying 'Miss, Miss,' as though he couldn't understand why I was leaving.

"He was like so many of the Indian men you see on the streets in St. James, slender fellows in narrow-waisted trousers and open-necked shirts. Ordinary, even with the good looks. But he had that special idea of beauty.

"That idea of beauty, surprising as it was, was not a secret. Many people would have known about it—like the junior teacher who had brought his name up at the staff meeting, and then didn't know how to describe him. He would have been used to people treating him in a special way: the women in the classes clapping him, other people mocking him or scorning him, and people like me running away from him because he frightened us. He frightened me because I felt his feeling for beauty was like an illness; as though some unfamiliar, deforming virus had passed through his simple mother to him, and was even then—he was in his mid-thirties—something neither of them had begun to understand."

"Prelude: An Inheritance" from *A Way in the World: A Novel*
by V. S. Naipaul

← Response notes →

This was what I heard, and the teacher couldn't tell me what had happened to Leonard Side; she had never thought to ask. Perhaps he had joined the great migration to England or the United States. I wondered whether in that other place Leonard Side had come to some understanding of his nature; or whether the thing that had frightened the teacher had, when the time of revelation came, also frightened Leonard Side.

He knew he was a Mohammedan, in spite of the picture of Christ in his bedroom. But he would have had almost no idea of where he or his ancestors had come from. He wouldn't have guessed that the name Side might have been a version of Sayed, and that his grandfather or great-grandfather might have come from a Shia Muslim group in India. From Lucknow, perhaps; there was even a street in St. James called Lucknow Street. All Leonard Side would have known of himself and his ancestors would have been what he had awakened to in his mother's house in St. James. In that he was like the rest of us.

With learning now I can tell you more or less how we all came to be where we were. I can tell you that the Amerindian name for that land of St. James would have been Cumucurapo, which the early travellers from Europe turned to Conquerabo or Conquerabia. I can look at the vegetation and tell you what was there when Columbus came and what was imported later. I can reconstruct the plantations that were laid out on that area of St. James. The recorded history of the place is short, three centuries of depopulation followed by two centuries of resettlement. The documents of the resettlement are available in the city, in the Registrar-General's Office. While the documents last we can hunt up the story of every strip of occupied land.

I can give you that historical bird's eye view. But I cannot really explain the mystery of Leonard Side's inheritance. Most of us know the parents or grandparents we come from. But we go back and back, forever; we go back all of us to the very beginning; in our blood and bone and brain we carry the memories of thousands of beings. I might say that an ancestor of Leonard Side's came from the dancing groups of Lucknow, the lewd men who painted their faces and tried to live like women. But that would only be a fragment of his inheritance, a fragment of the truth. We cannot understand all the traits we have inherited. Sometimes we can be strangers to ourselves.

👀 With a partner, discuss "Prelude: An Inheritance" and Naipaul's comment about not being born one's self. Naipaul suggests that history and inheritance are different. What does that mean? Do you agree? What does knowing our inheritance have to do with knowing ourselves? Write your responses.

Explore Naipaul's last line, "Sometimes we can be strangers to ourselves." Agree or disagree using examples from the text and your own experience.

Understanding the author's background and beliefs helps readers understand the meaning and ideas behind a story.

Naipaul has traveled all over the world during his life, writing about the people he sees and how they live. Yet, the more he has traveled, the more he has found himself focusing on people who are like him. He explains this in the Author's Foreword to *Finding the Center:* "A writer after a time carries his world with him, his own burden of experience, human experience and literary experience (one deepening the other) . . . ." Read how Naipaul describes his experiences of traveling.

from ***Finding the Center*** by V. S. Naipaul

← Response notes →

When more than twenty years ago I began to travel as a writer, I was uneasy and uncertain. My instinct was towards fiction; I found it constricting to have to deal with fact. I was glamored by the idea of the long journey, but I had no idea how I might set about looking at a place in a way that would be of value to other people. My brief—which was to look at various colonial territories in the Caribbean and South America—was political-cultural in intention. But I had no views or opinions, no system. I was interested in history; but I was also interested in landscape; above all, I was interested—at times frivolously—in people as I found them.

When it came to the writing, I was uncertain about the value I should give to the traveler's "I." This kind of direct participation came awkwardly to me, and the literary problem was also partly a personal one. In 1960 I was still a colonial, traveling to far-off places that were still colonies, in a world still more or less ruled by colonial ideas. In Surinam in 1961, in a banana plantation (curiously quiet, the mulch of rotting banana trash thick and soft and muffling underfoot), the Indian official who—with a Dutch technical expert in attendance—was showing me around broke off to say in a semiconspiratorial way, "You are the first one of us to come out on a mission like this."

To travel was glamorous. But travel also made unsuspected demands on me as a man and a writer, and perhaps for that reason it soon became a necessary stimulus for me. It broadened my world view; it showed me a changing world and took me out of my own colonial shell; it became the substitute for the mature social experience—the deepening knowledge of a society—which my background and the nature of my life denied me. My uncertainty about my role withered; a role was not necessary. I recognized my own instincts as a traveler and was content to be myself, to be what I had always been, a looker. And I learned to look in my own way.

To arrive at a place without knowing anyone there, and sometimes without an introduction; to learn how to move among strangers for the short time one could afford to be among them; to hold oneself in constant readiness for adventure or revelation; to allow oneself to be carried along, up to a point, by accidents; and consciously to follow up other impulses—that could be as creative and imaginative a procedure as the writing that came after. Travel of this sort became an intense experience for me. It used all the sides of my personality; I was always wound up. There were no rules. Every place visited was different; every place opened in a new way. Always, at the beginning, there was the possibility of failure—of not finding anything, not getting started on the chain of accidents and encounters. This gave a gambler's excitement to every arrival. My luck held; perhaps I made it hold. Always, after the tension, there came a moment when a place began to clear up and certain incidents (some of them disregarded until then) began to have meaning.

←—Response notes—→

In this excerpt Naipaul reveals some of his attitudes and opinions—some directly, some indirectly. To understand his ideas, focus on what he reveals about himself. List several of his attitudes and opinions below, labeling each one by how it is stated, (D) for direct or (I) for indirect.

example: *Travel became exciting because it broadened his world view* (D)

- ....

211

- ....

- ....

- ....

- ....

Naipaul liked traveling because he had always been "a looker." But he also knows that writing about his travels requires more than looking. He wrote, "However creatively one travels, however deep an experience in childhood or middle age, it takes thought (a sifting of impulses, ideas, and references that become more multifarious as one grows older) to understand what one has lived through or where one has been."

●❖ Describe an incident in your life that you now understand differently than when it first occurred. It may be about something you saw when you were traveling, but it does not have to be. Perhaps you walked around and saw something that you did not completely understand at first. Later, when you thought about it, you realized what you had "lived through."

To write realistically about experiences, writers must be able to express to the reader the significance of the events.

Five
A Portrait of the Writer

Much of Naipaul's writing defies classification. He mixes autobiography, fiction, and journalism. His description of the origins of his first book, *Miguel Street*, shows how he crafts his work.

from "A Prologue to an Autobiography," from ***Finding the Center***
by V. S. Naipaul

←—*Response notes*—→

Every morning when he got up Hat would sit on the banister of his back verandah and shout across, "What happening there, Bogart?" Luck was with me, because that first sentence was so direct, so uncluttered, so without complications, that it provoked the sentence that was to follow. *Bogart would turn in his bed and mumble softly, so that no one heard, "What happening there, Hat?"*

The first sentence was true. The second was invention. But together—to me, the writer—they had done something extraordinary. Though they had left out everything—the setting, the historical time, the racial and social complexities of the people concerned—they had suggested it all; they had created the world of the street. And together, as sentences, words, they had set up a rhythm, a speed, which dictated all that was to follow.

213

●◆ Reread the previous selections to find one or two examples of sentences that "set up a rhythm, a speed which dictated" what followed. Write the sentences below and explain why you think they explain "all that was to follow."

●◆ Write a sketch of Naipaul the writer. You will probably need to combine truth and invention, as Naipaul does. Imagine that you are writing to introduce him to someone who is completely unfamiliar with his work.

Knowing
how a writer describes the
act of writing can help you
understand his or her intentions
in writing.

Poetry Workshop

Talking About Poetry

To talk and to write about poems, you need to understand some of the terms used to describe them.

RHYTHM Recurrent sound in poetry is called rhythm. A poem can have a regular or irregular rhythm. The rhythm of a regular poem is referred to as meter.

METER The pattern of stressed and unstressed syllables in a line of poetry is called meter.

LINE Poetry is broken into lines which contain a varying number of words. Metrical lines are broken into units called feet and referred to by the number of feet:

- monometer: a line having one foot
- dimeter: a line having two feet
- trimeter: a line having three feet
- tetrameter: a line having four feet
- pentameter: a line having five feet
- hexameter: a line having six feet

FOOT The basic unit of a metrical line is the foot. It is a combination of two or three stressed and unstressed syllables. The basic feet are the following:

- iamb: an unstressed syllable followed by a stressed syllable
  (examples "below" "He ought")
- trochee: a stressed syllable followed by an unstressed syllable
  (examples "falling" "grown-up")
- anapest: two unstressed syllables followed by a stressed syllable
  (examples "intervene" "through the air")
- dactyl: a stressed syllable followed by two unstressed syllables
  (examples "yesterday" "A is for")
- spondee: two stressed syllables
  (examples "daybreak" "knock, knock")

RHYME The similarity or likeness of sound between two words is called rhyme. *Sat* and *cat* are a perfect rhyme because the vowel sounds and the final consonant of each word match exactly. Rhymes in which these do not exactly match (for example *room/storm* or *chill/fell*) are known as half-rhymes.

End rhyme (rhyme between the last word of two lines of poetry) is the most common in English, but there are many examples of internal rhyme (rhyme between words in a single line).

STANZA A group of lines that are set off to form a division in a poem is called a stanza. A stanza roughly makes up a unit of thought. In a metrical poem, the first stanza should set the pattern of the rhythm and rhyme. A two-line stanza is called a couplet. A three-line stanza is a tercet. A four-line stanza is called a quatrain.

215

Understanding the Rhyme

To determine the rhyme scheme of a poem (or stanza), underline the last word of each line. Use a small letter *a* to mark the sound of the first line. Every end word that has that sound will be an *a*. Use *b* for the next rhyming end word that has a different sound. Below, the rhyme scheme is marked on the opening lines of "Design" by Robert Frost as an example.

I found a dimpled spider, fat and <u>white</u>,	a
On a white heal-all, holding up a <u>moth</u>	b
Like a white piece of rigid satin <u>cloth</u>—	b
Assorted characters of death and <u>blight</u>	a
Mixed ready to begin the morning <u>right</u>,	a

Understanding Rhythm in Poetry

One of the most important but also most difficult things to do when studying poetry, is to hear the rhythm of a poem. It is important because it is one of the best ways to understand the poet's art. It is difficult because scanning lines—that is, determining where the stresses fall and what the meter of the line is—takes a lot of practice.

The first thing to remember is that poetry is an oral art. Stresses are determined by how a poem is read aloud. Robert Frost wrote in one of his letters, "The ear does it. The ear is the only true writer and the only true reader." Read the following lines from Frost's "Design" aloud and concentrate on the rhythm.

What had that flower to do with being white,
The wayside blue and innocent heal-all?
What brought the kindred spider to that height,
Then steered the white moth thither in the night?

The lines above are in iambic pentameter. The second and third lines are almost perfectly metrical. Below, the stressed syllables on the second line are marked by a / and unstressed ones by a ˘.

```
    ˘    /      /     /     ˘    /    ˘    /      /    /
 | The way | side blue | and in | no cent | heal-all |
```

The meter of this is iambic, but not every foot is an iamb. The second and fifth feet are spondees. Spondaic substitution is very common in lines of iambic pentameter.

Poets vary the meter to stress words or ideas and to keep the rhythm from growing boring. Note the substitution in the last foot of the following line:

```
 ˘        /      ˘   /    ˘   /    ˘  /    /   /
| What brought | the kin | dred spi | der to | that height |
```

Frost uses the first and last feet to maintain the iambic pattern, but puts great stress on the words "kindred spider." It emphasizes Frost's theme in the poem, the relationship between all things.

When you want to figure out the meter of a poem, begin by breaking a line into feet to determine the length. Then try to figure out the basic metrical foot of the line. One of the most important clues in scanning is verse form. Many poems are written in traditional verse forms that follow certain rules for the meter.

Recognizing Verse Forms

Some of the common verse forms in English are:

BLANK VERSE a verse form consisting of unrhymed iambic pentameter lines. It is the verse form closest to spoken English. Shakespeare's dramas were mostly written in blank verse.

COUPLET two lines of poetry with the same meter that often rhyme. "I am his Highness' dog at Kew; / Pray tell me, Sir, whose dog are you?" (Alexander Pope)

217

FREE VERSE poetry without any regular rhythm.

LIMERICK a five-line stanza usually rhyming *aabba*, with the first, second, and fifth lines written in trimeter and the third and fourth in dimeter. The limerick is generally witty and nonsensical.

ODE a lyric poem addressed to a person or subject. The ode is an ancient form that is often used as a commemoration or celebration.

SONNET a poem consisting of 14 lines of iambic pentameter. It is one of the most popular verse forms in English. There are two main types of sonnets, distinguished by the rhyme schemes and structure: the Italian sonnet and the Shakespearean sonnet.

- Italian sonnet (also known as the Petrarchan), a 14-line poem broken into two parts—an octave (eight lines) and a sestet (six lines)—usually rhyming *abbaabba cdecde*. The general structure of an Italian sonnet is to present a question or situation in the octave that is then resolved or commented on in the sestet.

- Shakesperean sonnet (also known as the Elizabethan), a 14-line poem consisting of three quatrains and a final couplet. The rhyme scheme is *abab cdcd efef gg*. Usually, the quatrains set forth a question or conflict that is answered or resolved in the couplet.

VILLANELLE a complex and highly-musical verse form that consists of five tercets rhyming *aba*, with a final quatrain rhyming *abaa*. The first line is used again as the sixth, twelfth, and eigtheenth lines. The third line is used again as the ninth, fifteenth, and nineteenth lines.

abstract, existing only as an idea, condition, or feeling that cannot be seen, heard, or touched. Something that is abstract is not CONCRETE.

alliteration, the repetition of the same initial sound in two or more nearby words in poetry or prose. "When to the sessions of sweet silent thought." (William Shakespeare, Sonnet 30) (See ASSONANCE and CONSONANCE.)

allusion, a reference in a literary work to a familiar person, place or thing.

annotation, a note or comment added to a text to question, explain, or critique the text.

antithesis, a FIGURE OF SPEECH that uses an opposition or contrast of ideas for effect. "It was the best of times, it was the worst of times. . . ." (Dickens, *A Tale of Two Cities*)

argument, the ideas or reasoning that hold together a work of literature.

assonance, the repetition of the same vowel sounds in two or more nearby words in poetry or prose. Assonance is similar to ALLITERATION, but not confined to the initial sound in a word. "That dolphin-torn, that gong-tormented sea." (W. B. Yeats, "Byzantium") (See CONSONANCE.)

audience, those people who read or hear what an author has written.

autobiography, an author's account of his or her own life. (See BIOGRAPHY and MEMOIR.)

biography, the story of a person's life written by another person. (See AUTOBIOGRAPHY.)

blank verse*, a VERSE FORM consisting of unrhymed IAMBIC PENTAMETER lines. It is the verse form closest to spoken English. Most of Shakespeare's dramas were mostly written in blank verse. (See RHYME.)

central idea, see MAIN IDEA.

characterization, the method an author uses to describe characters and their personalities.

concrete, existing as an actual object that can be seen, heard, or touched. Something that is concrete is not ABSTRACT.

conflict, the problem or struggle in a story that triggers the action. Conflict can be external (a character facing society, another chatacter, or a physical challenge) or internal (a character facing opposing forces within him- or herself).

consonance, the repetition of the same consonant sound before or after different vowels in two or more nearby words in poetry or prose. It is similar to ALLITERATION, but not confined to the initial sound in a word. "Courage was mine, and I had mystery / Wisdom was mine, and I had mastery." (Wilfred Owen, "Strange Meeting") (See ASSONANCE.)

couplet*, two LINES of poetry with the same METER and which often RHYME. "I am his Highness' dog at Kew; / Pray tell me, Sir, whose dog are you?" (Alexander Pope)

description, writing that paints a colorful picture of a person, place, thing, or idea using CONCRETE, vivid DETAILS.

detail, words from a DESCRIPTION that elaborate on subjects, characters, or action in a work. Details are generally vivid, colorful, and appeal to the senses.

dialect, a form of speech characteristic of a class or region and differing from the standard language in pronunciation, vocabulary, and grammatical form. The imitation of this regional speech in literature requires the use of altered, phonetic spellings.

dialogue, conversation carried on by the characters in a literary work.

diction, an author's choice of words in a literary work.

dimeter*, one of the metric lines of poetry. A LINE with two feet is in dimeter. (See METER and FOOT.)

dramatic monologue, a literary work (or part of one) in which a character is speaking as if another person were present. The speaker's words reveal something important about his or her character, or comments on the action.

emulation, a copy or IMITATION of a piece of literature, done to practice and study the style of the original.

essay, a type of NONFICTION in which ideas on a single topic are explained, argued, explored, and described. The essay is an immensely varied FORM.

fact, a thing known to be true or to have actually happened. (See OPINION.)

fairy tale, a type of FOLK LITERATURE, generally concerned with the supernatural adventures of a hero or heroine. Fairy tales are characterized by happy endings.

fiction, PROSE writing that tells an imaginary story. (See NOVEL and SHORT STORY.)

218

* See Poetry Workshop (pages 215–217)

figurative language, language used to create a special effect or feeling. It is characterized by FIGURES OF SPEECH or language that compares, exaggerates, or means something other than what it first appears to mean.

figures of speech, literary devices used to create special effects or feelings by making comparisons. The most common types are ALLITERATION, ANTITHESIS, HYPERBOLE, METAPHOR, METONYMY, PERSONIFICATION, REPETITION, SIMILE, and UNDERSTATEMENT.

first-person narrator, See POINT OF VIEW.

foot*, the basic unit of METER. It is a combination of two or three stressed and unstressed syllables. The most common feet are the IAMB and the TROCHEE. (See STRESS.)

foreshadowing, hints about what is going to happen, given by the writer to the reader.

form, the structure or organization a writer uses for a literary work. There are a large number of possible forms, including fable, parable, romance, and parody. (See VERSE FORM.)

free verse*, poetry that does not have a regular METER or a RHYME scheme.

generalization, an idea or statement that emphasizes the general characteristics rather than the specific details of a subject.

genre, a category or type of literature based on its style, form, and content. The major genres are DRAMA, FICTION, NONFICTION, and POETRY.

hexameter*, one of the metric lines of poetry. A LINE with six feet is in hexameter. (See METER and FOOT.)

hyperbole, a FIGURE OF SPEECH that uses exaggeration, or overstatement, for effect. "I have seen this river so wide it had only one bank." (Mark Twain, *Life on the Mississippi*)

iamb*, a metrical FOOT in poetry. It consists of a unstressed syllable followed by a stressed one. *New York* and *repeat* are examples of iambs. (See METER and STRESS.)

imagery, the words or phrases a writer uses to represent objects, feelings, actions, or ideas. Imagery is usually based on sensory DETAILS.

imitation, a piece of literature consciously modeled after an earlier piece. An imitations can be a copy done for practice or a serious homage to a writer. (See EMULATION.)

inference, a reasonable conclusion about a character or event in a literary work drawn from the limited facts made available.

inflection, a change in the tone or the pitch of the voice. The inflection of the voice implies the use of a word. The word *well* can be used as an adjective, noun, or exclamation and is inflected differently with each use.

irony, the use of a word or phrase to mean the exact opposite of its literal or normal meaning.

Italian sonnet* (also known as the Petrarchan), a 14-LINE poem broken into two parts—an octave (eight lines) and a sestet (six lines)—usually rhyming *abbaabba cdecde*. The general structure of an Italian sonnet is to present a question in the octave that is resolved in the sestet. (See RHYME and SONNET.)

journal, a daily record of thoughts, impressions, and autobiographical information. A journal can be a source of ideas for writing.

limited narrator, a THIRD-PERSON NARRATOR who is telling a story from one character's POINT OF VIEW. (See OMNISCIENT NARRATOR.)

line*, the metric form of POETRY, which is generally distinguished from PROSE by being broken into lines. Lines are named according to the number of feet they contain and the pattern of these feet. The principal line lengths are MONOMETER, DIMETER, TRIMETER, TETRAMETER, PENTAMETER, and HEXAMETER. (See METER and FOOT.)

literal, the actual or dictionary meaning of a word. It also refers to the common meaning of phrases, rather than the imaginative or implied meaning an author may add.

main idea, the central point or purpose in a work of literature. It is often stated in a thesis statement or topic sentence. Main idea is more commonly employed in discussing NONFICTION than the other GENRES.

memoir, a type of AUTOBIOGRAPHY that generally focuses on a specific subject or period rather than the complete story of the author's life.

metaphor, a FIGURE OF SPEECH in which one thing is described in terms of another. The comparison is usually indirect, unlike a SIMILE in which it is direct. "My thoughts are sheep, which I both guide and serve." (Sir Philip Sidney's, *Arcadia*)

meter*, the pattern of stressed and unstressed syllables in a LINE of poetry. The basic unit of meter is the FOOT. (See STRESS.)

metonymy, a FIGURE OF SPEECH that substitutes one word for another that is closely related. "The White House has decided to provide a million more public service jobs" is an example. *White House* is substituting for *president*.

219

monometer*, one of the metric lines of poetry. A LINE with one FOOT is in monometer. (See METER.)

mood, the feeling a piece of literature arouses in the reader. It is reflected by the overall atmosphere of the work. (See TONE.)

myth, a traditional story connected with the beliefs of a culture.

narrative, writing or speaking that tells a story or recounts an event.

narrator, the person telling the story in a work of literature. (See LIMITED NARRATOR, OMNISCIENT NARRATOR, and POINT OF VIEW.)

nonfiction, prose writing that tells a true story or explores an idea. There are many categories of nonfiction, including AUTOBIOGRAPHY, BIOGRAPHY, and ESSAY. (See GENRE.)

novel, a lengthy fictional story with a plot that is revealed by the speech, action, and thoughts of the characters. Novels differ from SHORT STORIES by being developed in much greater depth and detail. (See FICTION and GENRE.)

objective, refers to NONFICTION writing that relates information in an impersonal manner; without feelings or opinions. (See SUBJECTIVE.)

220 ode, a VERSE FORM that is generally a formal address in commemoration or celebration of a person, event, or idea. The ode is one of the oldest verse forms in existence.

omniscient narrator, a THIRD-PERSON NARRATOR who is able to see into the minds of all the characters in a literary work, narrating the story from multiple POINTS OF VIEW. (See LIMITED NARRATOR.)

opinion, what one thinks or believes. An opinion is generally based on knowledge, but it is not a FACT.

pentameter*, one of the metric lines of poetry. A LINE with five feet is in pentameter. (See METER and FOOT.)

personification, a FIGURE OF SPEECH in which an author embodies an inanimate object with human characteristics. "The rock stubbornly refused to move" is an example.

perspective, See POINT OF VIEW.

plot, the action or sequence of events in a story. It is usually a series of related incidents that build upon one another as the story develops.

poetry*, a GENRE of writing that is an imaginative response to experience reflecting a keen awareness of language. Poetry is generally characterized by LINES, RHYTHM and, often, RHYME.

point of view, literary term for the perspective from which a story is told. In the first-person point of view, the story is told by one of the characters: "I was tired so I took the shortcut through the cemetery." In the third-person point of view, the story is told by someone outside the story: "The simple fact is that he lacked confidence. He would rather do something he wasn't that crazy about doing than risk looking foolish." A third-person narrator can be LIMITED or OMNISCIENT. (See NARRATOR.)

prose, writing or speaking in the usual or ordinary form. Prose is any form of writing that is not POETRY.

quatrain*, a STANZA of four LINES. The lines can be in any METER or RHYME scheme.

refrain, the repetition of a line or phrase of a poem at regular intervals, especially at the end of each STANZA. A song's refrain is known as a chorus.

repetition, a FIGURE OF SPEECH in which a word, phrase, or idea is repeated for emphasis and rhythmic effect in a piece of literature. "Bavarian gentians, big and dark, only dark / darkening the day-time, torch-like with the smoking blueness of Pluto's gloom." (D. H. Lawrence, "Bavarian Gentians")

rhyme*, the similarity or likeness of sound existing between two words. *Sat* and *cat* are a perfect rhyme because the vowel sounds and final consonant of each word match exactly. Rhyme is a characteristic of POETRY.

rhythm*, the ordered occurrence of sound in POETRY. Regular rhythm is called METER. Poetry without regular rhythm is called FREE VERSE.

satire, is a literary TONE used to ridicule or make fun of human vice or weakness. Satire is often used with the intent of correcting the subject of the attack.

scene, See SETTING.

setting, the time and place in which the action of a literary work occurs.

Shakespearean sonnet* (also known as the Elizabethan), a 14-LINE poem consisting of three QUATRAINS and a final COUPLET. The rhyme scheme is *abab cdcd efef gg*. Usually, the quatrains set forth a question or conflict that is answered or resolved in the couplet. (See RHYME and SONNET.)

short story, a brief fictional story. It usually contains one major theme and one major character. (See FICTION, GENRE, and NOVEL.)

* See Poetry Workshop (pages 215–217)

simile, a FIGURE OF SPEECH in which one thing is likened to another. It is a direct comparison employing the words *like* or *as*. Cicero's "A room without books is like a body without a soul" is an example. (See METAPHOR.)

slang, word uses that are not part of the formal language, but carry a particular vividness or coloring. Slang words appear and fade with great speed.

sonnet*, a poem consisting of 14 LINES of IAMBIC PENTAMETER. It is one of the most popular VERSE FORMS in English. There are two main types of sonnets distinguished by their RHYME schemes and structure: the ITALIAN SONNET and the SHAKESPEAREAN SONNET.

stanza*, a group of LINES that are set off to form a division in POETRY. A two-line stanza is called a COUPLET. A four-line stanza is a QUATRAIN.

stream of consciousness, a style of writing in which a character's thoughts and feelings are recorded as they occur. Images, memories, and ideas occur in a seemingly random fashion as the writer tries to imitate the way people perceive things.

stress*, the vocal emphasis given a syllable or word in a metrical pattern. (See METER.)

structure, See FORM.

style, how an author uses words, phrases, and sentences to form ideas. Style is the qualities and characteristics that distinguish one writer's work from another's.

subjective, NONFICTION writing that includes personal feelings, attitudes, or OPINIONS. (See OBJECTIVE.)

symbol, a person, place, thing, or event used to represent something else. The *dove* is a symbol of peace. Characters in literature are often symbolic of an idea.

syntax, sentence structure; the order and relationship of words in a sentence.

tetrameter*, one of the metric lines of poetry. A LINE with four feet is in tetrameter. (See METER and FOOT.)

theme, the statement about life that a writer is trying to get across in a piece of writing. Lengthy pieces may have several themes. In stories written for children, the theme is generally spelled out at the end. In more complex literature, the theme is implied.

thesis, a statement of purpose, intent, or MAIN IDEA in a literary work.

third-person narrator, See POINT OF VIEW.

tone, a writer's attitude toward the subject. A writer's tone can be serious, sarcastic, solemn, OBJECTIVE, and so on.

tradition, the inherited past that is available to an author to study and learn from. This generally includes language, the body of literature, FORMS, and conventions.

trimeter*, one of the metric lines of poetry. A LINE with three feet is in trimeter. (See METER and FOOT.)

trochee*, a metrical FOOT in poetry. It consists of a stressed syllable followed by an unstressed one. *Falling* and *older* are examples of trochees. (See METER and STRESS.)

understatement, a FIGURE OF SPEECH that states an idea with restraint to emphasize what is being written about. The common usage of "Not bad" to mean *good* is an example of understatement.

verse form*, the form taken by the lines of a poem. Some of the common verse forms in English are BLANK VERSE, the COUPLET, the QUATRAIN, and the SONNET. (See LINE.)

villanelle*, a complex and highly-musical verse form that consists of five tercets rhyming *aba*, with a final quatrain rhyming *abaa*. The first line is used again as the sixth, twelfth, and eigtheenth lines. The third line is used again as the ninth, fifteenth, and nineteenth lines.

voice, an author's distinctive style and unique way of expressing ideas.

221

10 "Mother, Summer, I" from *Collected Poems* by Philip Larkin. Copyright © 1988, 1989 by the Estate of Philip Larkin. Reprinted by permission of Farrar, Straus & Giroux, Inc.

11 "Far Out" from *Collected Poems* by Philip Larkin. Copyright © 1988, 1989 by the Estate of Philip Larkin. Reprinted by permission of Farrar, Straus & Giroux, Inc.

12 "Ambulances" from *Collected Poems* by Philip Larkin. Copyright © 1988, 1989 by the Estate of Philip Larkin. Reprinted by permission of Farrar, Straus & Giroux, Inc.

16 "Street Lamps" from *Collected Poems* by Philip Larkin. Copyright © 1988, 1989 by the Estate of Philip Larkin. Reprinted by permission of Farrar, Straus & Giroux, Inc.

18, 19 Excerpts from the notebooks of Philip Larkin from *Philip Larkin: A Writer's Life* by Andrew Motion © 1993 Andrew Motion. Used by permission of Andrew Motion and the Estate of Philip Larkin.

22 From *Paddy Clarke Ha Ha Ha* by Roddy Doyle. Copyright © 1933 by Roddy Doyle. Used by permission of Viking Penguin, a division of Penguin Putnam Inc. and Martin Secker & Warburg, U.K.

26 Excerpt from "The Piano Tuner's Wives" from *After Rain* by William Trevor. Copyright © 1996 by William Trevor. Used by permission of Viking Penguin, a division of Penguin Putnam Inc.

30 Excerpt from *The Conversations at Curlow Creek* by David Malouf. Copyright © 1996 by David Malouf. Reprinted by permission of Pantheon Books, a division of Random House, Inc.

36 Excerpt from *Listening for Small Sounds* by Penelope Trevor. First published in 1996 by Allen & Unwin Pty Ltd., NSW, Australia. Reprinted by permission of the publisher, Allen & Unwin.

38 "Comrades" by Nadine Gordimer. First published in *Interview Magazine*.

43 "An Iff and a Butt," from *Haroun and the Sea of Stories* by Salman Rushdie. Copyright © 1990 by Salman Rushdie. Used by permission of Viking Penguin, a division of Penguin Putnam Inc.

50 Excerpt from "Subterranean Gothic," copyright © 1984 by Paul Theroux, first printed in *Granta* Magazine. Reprinted by permission of the Wylie Agency, Inc..

52, 55 Excerpts from "Sea-Room" by Jonathan Raban. Copyright © 1984 Jonathan Raban reprinted with the permission of Aitken & Stone Ltd.

57 Excerpt from *When the Going was Good* by Evelyn Waugh. Copyright © 1934, 1962 by Evelyn Waugh. By permission of Little, Brown and Company.

59 Excerpt from *Bury Me Standing* by Isabel Fonseca. Copyright © 1995 by Isabel Fonseca. Reprinted by permission of Alfred A. Knopf Inc.

63 *Missing* from *Daughters and Rebels* by Jessica Mitford. Copyright © 1960 by Jessica Treuhaft. Reprinted by permission of the author. All rights reserved.

65, 68 Excerpts from "Great Men's Houses" from *The London Scene* by Virginia Woolf. Copyright © 1975 by Angelica Garnett and Quentin Bell. Reprinted by permission of Random House, Inc., Executors of the Virginia Woolf estate, and Hogarth Press.

71 "Telephone Conversation" by Wole Soyinka, first published in *Reflections: Nigerian Prose and Verse*, edited by Frances Ademola. Copyright © 1962 Wole Soyinka. Reprinted by permission of Wole Soyinka.

73 "The Virgins" from *Sea Grapes* by Derek Walcott. Copyright © 1976 by Derek Walcott. Reprinted by permission of Farrar, Straus & Giroux, Inc. and Jonathan Cape, London.

76 "Hawk Roosting" from *New and Selected Poems* by Ted Hughes. Copyright © 1982 by Ted Hughes. Reprinted by permission of HarperCollins Publishers, Inc.

79 "I Think Continually Of" from *Collected Poems 1928-1953* by Stephen Spender. Copyright © 1934 and renewed 1962 by Stephen Spender. Reprinted by permission of Random House, Inc.

81 "To an Athlete Dying Young" from *The Collected Poems of A. E. Housman*. Copyright 1939, 1940, © 1965 by Henry Holt and Company, Inc., © 1967, 1968 by Robert E. Symons. Reprinted by permission of Henry Holt and Company, Inc.

83 "Naming of Parts" from *Lessons of the War* by Henry Reed. Reprinted from *Collected Poems* (1991) by Henry Reed, edited by Jon Stallworthy. By permission of Oxford University Press.

88 "Fern Hill" from *The Poems of Dylan Thomas*. Copyright © 1945 by the Trustees for the Copyrights of Dylan Thomas. Reprinted by permission of New Directions Publishing Corp.

93, 96, 98 Excerpts from *A Portrait of the Artist as a Young Man* by James Joyce. Reprinted by permission of the Estate of James Joyce.

102 "The Wild Swans at Coole" from *The Collected Works of W. B. Yeats, Volume I: The Poems*. Revised and edited by Richard J. Finneran (New York: Scribner, 1997). Copyright © 1924 by Macmillan Publishing Company, renewed 1952 by Bertha Georgie Yeats. Reprinted with the permission of Scribner, a Division of Simon & Schuster.

104 "Coole Park, 1929" from *The Collected Works of W. B. Yeats, Volume I: The Poems*. Revised and edited by Richard J. Finneran (New York: Scribner, 1997). Copyright © 1924 by Macmillan Publishing Company, renewed 1952 by Bertha Georgie Yeats. Reprinted with the permission of Scribner, a Division of Simon & Schuster.

106 "The Second Coming" from *The Collected Works of W. B. Yeats, Volume I: The Poems*. Revised and edited by Richard J. Finneran (New York: Scribner, 1997). Copyright © 1924 by Macmillan Publishing Company, renewed 1952 by Bertha Georgie Yeats. Reprinted with the permission of Scribner, a Division of Simon & Schuster.

109 "What Then?" from *The Collected Works of W. B. Yeats, Volume I: The Poems*. Revised and edited by Richard J. Finneran (New York: Scribner, 1997). Copyright © 1924 by Macmillan Publishing Company, renewed 1952 by Bertha Georgie Yeats. Reprinted with the permission of Scribner, a Division of Simon & Schuster.

111 Excerpt from the Introduction to *The Oxford Book of Modern Verse*. Copyright © 1936. Reprinted by permission of Oxford University Press.

114 "Trail of the Green Blazer" from *Malgudi Days* by R. K. Narayan. Copyright © 1972, 1975, 1978, 1980, 1981, 1982 by R. K. Narayan. Used by permission of Viking Penguin, a division of Penguin Putnam Inc.

119 "Homage for Isaac Babel" from *Stories* by Doris Lessing. Copyright © 1978 Doris Lessing. Reprinted by kind permission of Alfred A. Knopf, Inc. and Jonathan Clowes Ltd., London, on behalf of Doris Lessing.

123 Excerpt from "Writing a Story—One Man's Way" from *A Frank O'Connor Reader*, edited by Michael Steinman. Reprinted by permission of Syracuse University Press.

126 *Missing* from *Birdsong* by Sebastian Faulks. Copyright © 1993 by Sebastian Faulks. Used with permission of Hutchinson Publishing, a division of Random House UK, London.

131 Excerpt from "England, My England" from *The Complete Short Stories of D. H. Lawrence*. Copyright 1922 by Thomas Seltzer, Inc. Renewal copyright 1950 by Frieda Lawrence. Used by permission of Viking Penguin, a division of Penguin Putnam Inc.

132 Excerpt from *The Unicorn* by Iris Murdoch. Copyright © 1963, 1991 by Iris Murdoch. Used by permission of Viking Penguin, a division of Penguin Putnam Inc.

134 Excerpt from Family and Friends by Anita Brookner. Copyright © 1985 by Anita Brookner. Reprinted by permission of Pantheon Books, a division of Random House, Inc.

142 "Randolf's Party" from *In His Own Write* by John Lennon. Copyright © Yoko Ono. Reprinted by permission of the Estate of John Lennon.

144, 146 From *A Clockwork Orange* by Anthony Burgess. Copyright © 1962, 1989, renewed 1990 by Anthony Burgess. Reprinted by permission of W. W. Norton & Company, Inc. and Heinemann, U.K.

152 "Dulce et Decorum Est" from *The Collected Poems of Wilfred Owen*. Copyright © 1963 by Chatto & Windus, Ltd. Reprinted by permission of New Directions Publishing Corp.

154 Quotation by Patrick Kavanuagh reprinted by kind permission of the Trustees of the Estate of Patrick Kavanagh, c/o Peter Fallon, Literary Agent, Loughcrew, Oldcastle, Co. Meath, Ireland.

154 "The Reading Lesson" by Richard Murphy. Used by kind permission of the author.

156, 159 Excerpts from "On Seeing England for the First Time" by Jamaica Kincaid. First published in *Harper's Magazine*, August 1991. Reprinted by permission.

162 "Ireland 1972" by Paul Durcan. Used by permission of the author.

164, 169 Excerpts from "Greenhouse with Cyclamens—I" from *A Train of Powder* by Rebecca West. Reprinted by permission of The Peters Fraser and Dunlop Group Limited on behalf of the Estate of Rebecca West. © Rebecca West 1955.

172, 175 Excerpts from *An Experiment in Criticism* by C. S. Lewis. Copyright © 1961 by Cambridge University Press. Reprinted with the permission of Cambridge University Press.

178 "To My Mother" by George Barker from *Collected Poems by George Barker*, edited by Robert Fraser. Used by permission of Faber and Faber Ltd.

182, 184, 185 "In Memory of W. B. Yeats" by W. H. Auden. Reprinted from *W. H. Auden: Collected Poems*, edited by Edward Mendelson. Copyright © 1940 and renewed 1968 by W. H. Auden. Reprinted by permission of Random House, Inc.

194 "A Rhinoceros and a Lion" by Kaoru Maruyama, translated by Satoru Sato and Constance Udang. First appeared in *Poetry Magazine*, May 1956. Copyright © 1956 by The Modern Poetry Association. Reprinted by permission of the editor of *Poetry*.

196 Excerpt from "Burnt Norton" from *Four Quartets* by T. S. Eliot. Copyright © 1943 by T. S. Eliot and renewed 1971 by Esme Valerie Eliot. Reprinted by permission of Harcourt Brace & Company.

200 Excerpt from hat by V. S. Naipaul. Copyright © 1959 by V. S. Naipaul. Reprinted with the permission of Aitken & Stone Ltd.

202, 206 Excerpts from *A Way in the World: A Novel* by V. S. Naipaul. Copyright © 1994 by V. S. Naipaul. Reprinted by permission of Alfred A. Knopf Inc.

210, 213 Excerpts from *Finding the Center* by V. S. Naipaul. Copyright © 1984 by V. S. Naipaul. Reprinted by permission of Alfred A. Knopf Inc.

Every effort has been make to secure complete rights and permissions for each literary excerpt presented herein. Updated acknowledgements will appear in subsequent printings.

Design: Christine Ronan Design

Photographs: Unless otherwise noted below, all photographs are the copyrighted work of Mel Hill.

Front and Back cover: © John Brown/Tony Stone Images

9 © Peter Turnley/Corbis

21 © Terry Vine/Tony Stone Images

35 © /Tony Stone Images

49 © Gary Randall/FPG International

61 © Philip Condit II/Tony Stone Images

75 © John Zillioux/Gamma Liason International

87 © Hulton-Deutsch Collection/Corbis

101 © Paul Harris/Tony Stone Images

113 © Evan Evans/ibid, inc.

125 © Peter Brown/Peter Brown

139 © Nick Vaccaro/Photonica

151 © Manuela Hoefer/Tony Stone Images

163 © Anthony Suau/Gamma Liason International

177 © Mike McQueen/Tony Stone Images

187 © Genevieve Naylor/Corbis

199 © Joshua Sheldon/Photonica

Picture Research: Feldman and Associates

224